The publisher and the University of California Press Foundation
gratefully acknowledge the generous support of the Constance and
William Withey Endowment Fund in History and Music.

Camera Palæstina

Camera Palæstina

Photography and Displaced Histories of Palestine

Issam Nassar
Stephen Sheehi
Salim Tamari

UNIVERSITY OF CALIFORNIA PRESS

University of California Press
Oakland, California

Suggested citation: Nassar, I., Sheehi, S., and Tamari, S. *Camera Palæstina: Photography and Displaced Histories of Palestine.* Oakland: University of California Press, 2022. DOI: https://doi.org/10.1525/luminos.126

Library of Congress Cataloging-in-Publication Data

Names: Nassar, Issam, author. | Sheehi, Stephen, 1967– author. |
    Tamārī, Salīm, author.
Title: Camera Palæstina : photography and displaced histories of Palestine/
    Issam Nassar, Stephen Sheehi, Salīm Tamārī.
Description: Oakland, California : University of California Press, [2022] |
    Series: New directions in Palestinian studies ; 5 | Includes bibliographical
    references and index.
Identifiers: LCCN 2021042440 (print) | LCCN 2021042441 (ebook) |
    ISBN 9780520382886 (paperback) | ISBN 9780520382893 (ebook)
Subjects: LCSH: Jawharīyah, Wāṣif, 1897–1973. | Jerusalem—
    History—20th century—Pictorial works. | Palestine—History—
    20th century—Pictorial works. | Jerusalem—Description and travel. |
    Palestine—Description and travel.
Classification: LCC DS109.93 .N38 2022 (print) | LCC DS109.93 (ebook) |
    DDC 956.940022/2—dc23

LC record available at https://lccn.loc.gov/2021042440
LC ebook record available at https://lccn.loc.gov/2021042441

31 30 29 28 27 26 25 24 23 22
10 9 8 7 6 5 4 3 2 1

لذكرى واصف جوهرية وأهالي القدس التي عشقها

CONTENTS

LIST OF FIGURES

ACKNOWLEDGMENTS

We are grateful to the Jawhariyyeh family for making available copies of the four volumes of the original albums in Athens and their indices in Beirut. Aya Shaker Jawhariyyeh in Jerusalem was the first person to encourage the editing of the handwritten memoirs of her father. Wasif Jawhariyyeh in Amman, his grandfather's namesake, graciously expedited our access to the Athens Collection. Katy Jawhariyyeh kindly hosted us in her Glyfada home and patiently supervised the scanning process. In Beirut, we were fortunate to have full access to the Institute of Palestine Studies (IPS) collection over the last fifteen years, from the Director to the staff of the library and the photographic archive. Particular thanks go to Mona Nsouli (former director), Jeanette Saroufim (former head librarian), and Mirna Itani (archivist), who have been generous with their time, energy and expertise. They greatly facilitated our research during our many visits to Beirut as well as while we were abroad. Our gratitude goes to Hala Zeinelabidin, the head librarian, and the archival staff Nour Bahja, Rihab Sakr, Tamara Bourji, Salwa Jaradat, Yousef Naanaa, and Hadeel al-Ali. Hala Zeinelabidin was crucial in providing us with advice and high-quality images in the final stages of preparing the manuscript.

We extend a special and warm thanks to Beshara Doumani, the editor of New Directions in Palestinian Studies series. Not only did he graciously encourage us in the submission of the manuscript and facilitate its publication by the University of California Press, he generously followed up throughout the process of review, revisions, and production of the book, even after his appointment as President of Birzeit University. We not only appreciate his energies in contributing to Palestine Studies writ large but, more personally, we thank him for his friendship, honesty, and support.

Our sincere gratitude goes to the external evaluators and anonymous readers of the earliest submission of the proposal and of our final draft to the press. These scholars provided us with critical assessment, suggestions, and support that significantly improved the book. They aided us to think about how our three disciplinary methodologies integrate into a larger coherent project around the social history and photography of Palestine, while also sharing their enthusiasm for our vision.

At the University of California Press, we are indebted for the continued support of Niels Hooper. He remains an extraordinarily gracious and supportive editor, whose affable personality, keen intellect, and willingness to talk with us throughout the process made getting *Camera Palæstina* to print a collaborative pleasure. Likewise, this book would not be the same without the tireless and sustained attention of Naja Pulliam Collins. Her meticulous help, care, and sincerity in final preparation and production of manuscript was not only exemplary but heartfelt and meaningful to us.

Each of us thank our academic institutions and departments for providing financial support for travel to Beirut and various MESA conferences, where we three could meet in person to plan and discuss this book. Particularly, Istifan (Stephen Sheehi) acknowledges his research funds and professorship from the Sultan Qaboos Endowment to William & Mary as well as the supportive environment from the Asian and Middle East Studies Program, Modern Languages and Literature Department, and Asian and Pacific-Islander American Studies Program. Likewise, he thanks Eve Zimmerman and the Suzanne Newhouse Center for the Humanities for hosting him as the Mary L. Cornille Distinguished Professor of the Humanities at Wellesley College for part of the time that we were completing this monograph.

Finally, the generosity and friendship between we three authors made collaboration in organizing, researching, and writing this book a pleasure and truly a cooperative enterprise. Relatedly, we would like to thank our family and friends for their love and friendship over the past several years (including during the Covid-19 pandemic). Without their presence and affection, this book would have been impossible. It is their love that give us inspiration and motivation to continue to fight for the liberation of Palestine.

From the Series Editor

As Elias Sanbar once wrote, "Few countries have been photographed as much as Palestine." In the nineteenth and early twentieth centuries, colonial expansion brought European photographers into the Eastern Mediterranean and Southwest Asia. In Palestine this process in Palestine was driven in no small part by European interest in the "Holy Land." Photography's unique ability to capture the "truth" of Palestine, and to freeze it in time, was of particular interest to those who sought to verify the timeless truth of the Bible. It was not long, however, before local Arab and Armenian photographers—including Garabed Krikorian, Yesayi Garabedian, Khalil Raad, Daoud Saboungi, Issa Sawabini, and others—began documenting the people, places, and events of Palestine. In the first half of the twentieth century, Wasif Jawhariyyeh, a Jerusalemite musician and petty official in the British Mandate administration, collected nearly nine hundred photographs from both European and local photographers in seven albums, which he titled *Tarikh filastin al-musawwar*, or "The Illustrated History of Palestine."

Jawhariyyeh's collection of photographs is only one component of a larger assemblage. The photographs were numbered, captioned, and arranged in seven volumes, accompanied by three bound volumes of handwritten memoirs; a seventy-eight-page reference catalogue of the photograph albums; a fourteen-page index and summary of the reference catalogue; and a folder of unindexed photographs. But this collection was itself only part of a larger Jawhariyyeh Collection that Wasif assembled at his home in Jerusalem before 1948 and which included Palestinian and Arab art, textiles, furniture, musical instruments, and, of course, photographs. Jawhariyyeh's urge to collect and order—that is, to archive—foreshadows the "archive fever" prevalent among Palestinians in the past quarter-century.

How, then, to read this archive, this collection of photographs, which Jawhariyyeh did not take and in which he only rarely featured, but in which he clearly saw himself? What is the logic—or logics—that orders the albums? Are they a visual companion to Jawhariyyeh's written memoirs? Should they be read according to their handwritten index? Should they be read on their own, as a historical narrative that progresses for the most part chronologically through the first five volumes? Or did Jawhariyyeh arrange his albums as a musical piece, progressing from one movement to the next, with a musician's sense of rhythm and dynamics? Were they one exhibition in the Palestinian museum that Jawhariyyeh imagined himself building in his Jerusalem home? Such questions are larger than Jawhariyyeh and his albums, just as *Camera Palæstina* is more than an exploration of a single collection and the worldview of its collector. Rather, they invite us to re-read, reimagine, and re-orient (or disorient) the visual record of Ottoman and Mandate Palestine more broadly.

Even if we may find elements of melancholy in the albums, *Camera Palæstina* insists that we resist reading them through the lens of nostalgia for a Palestine before the Nakba. Instead of a record of a Palestine lost, Issam Nassar, Stephen Sheehi, and Salim Tamari suggest that Jawhariyyeh's albums and their contents illuminate Palestine as a lived and living social fact. This is a Palestine that was and is characterized by multiplicities and tensions, by dissonance as much as coherence. Jawhariyyeh's arrangement and labeling remind us that photographs are not mere visual "evidence" of a particular time-space, but are objects with social lives. These social lives arise out of the contexts and conditions of their production, their distribution, their collection, their presentation, and their viewing, and as each of these processes brings together different technologies, economies, social networks, and temporal imaginations. Jawhariyyeh's collection weaves together and negotiates multiple social and ideological positions. *Camera Palæstina* in turn explores its tensions without resolution.

The New Directions in Palestinian Studies (NDPS) book series centers Palestinian experiences and perspectives to illuminate their complexity and to explore the Palestinian condition as a site for producing theory. *Camera Palæstina* uses locally generated vernacular sources to assert an indigenous Palestinian visuality that refuses Palestinians' physical, historical, and visual negation by Orientalist, British colonial, and Zionist settler-colonial regimes. This is not simply a project of recovering the past. It is instead an exploration of Palestinians' living political, cultural, and social communities in the present and its lessons for decolonial approaches to photography, archives, museums, and knowledge production generally.

This book employs the Library of Congress transliteration system. We note differences in *'ayn* (') and *hamza* (') but do not use macros or diacritics to identify particular Arabic letters or differentiate long and short vowels. When using the definite article (al-), we do not distinguish between *qamari* and *shamsi* letters. Therefore, the definite article (*al-*) is contracted with the following definite article (e.g. *wa+al = wal*) We translate the *ta-marbutah* as *–ah* unless it is in an *idafa*, in which case it is *at*. For feminine *nisbah* adjectives, the book uses *–iyah*, not *iyya*.

Most transliterations should be clear even to readers without an advanced level of Arabic. We kept Anglicized versions of Arabic personal names when they have appeared within the Anglophone historical, academic or mainstream record (e.g. Jawhariyyeh, Safieh, Raad, and Husseini as opposed to Jawhariyah, Safiyah, R'ad, and Husayni) and popular Arab names in English, such as Abdallah/Abdullah, are provided without indicating the *'ayn*. The same is the case for particular types of place names, such as Beit Safafa as opposed to Bayt Safafa. We use the predominant English translation for well-known geographic locations, such as Palestine, Jerusalem, Cairo, Beirut, etc. When we use the indigenous Arabic place name, we gloss the Arabic with an English translation in parentheses the first time we mention that location (e.g., Bab al-Khalil [Jaffa Gate]).

Many Ottoman Turkish names remain Arabized, such as Jamal Pasha, although some are left in their Ottoman Turkish original, such as Abdülaziz and Abdülhamid.

All translations are our own unless otherwise indicated.

1

Ways of Seeing the Palestinian Visual Archive

The photographic oeuvre of Wasif Jawhariyyeh (1897–1968), if one may call it that, is no longer unknown. His albums, ostensibly titled *Tarikh Filistin al-musawwar* or the "Illustrated History of Palestine," have been explored by a number of different scholars in an array of venues, largely focusing on representing historic Palestine "before the diaspora."[1] With a large handful of notable exceptions, most of the images themselves, as we will see in this book, were produced by marquee indigenous and expatriate studios and, therefore, can be found elsewhere. As such, the photographic bricolage that structures these albums (individually and if approached as an *oeuvre* or an archive) makes us ponder both the "history of photography in Palestine" and "the history of Palestine through the photograph." Whether an *oeuvre*, an archive, or an individual enunciation, we are compelled to consider photographic collection and visual narration as an act, as a document and as a testimony. Rather than consider the "history of photography in Palestine" and "the history of Palestine through the photograph" as separate fields of inquiry, we posit that Wasif Jawhariyyeh's albums allow us to seek the confluence, overlaps, departures, tensions, and interplay between the two.

The most fundamental assertion of this book is that the juncture between the history of photography in Palestine and the history of Palestine through photography offers us evidence of the unbroken field of material, historical, and collective experience that constitutes an uncontestable continuum of what is Arab Palestine, from its living past to its living present. Here, we would argue against a nostalgic reading of Jawhariyyeh's photographs, a reading that suggests the loss and erasure of Palestine as a historical and present fact. Certainly, as Tamari's contribution shows, particular forms of melancholy may haunt these images or play a role in organizing their selection. "Haunting" is relational, however. Therefore, we indubitably acknowledge that the Zionist settler-colonial ethos is built on the erasure of the Palestinians from their homeland. This ethos has translated into a coordinated, sustained, and targeted program to forcefully remove Palestinians from their lands as readily as from history books and the visual field of the "Holy Land" itself. In this way, a melancholic reading or the invocation of haunting may do nothing to disrupt settler colonial futures.

The three readings presented here, while historical in nature, locate the *meaning* of the social life of photography in living Palestine. A reading and close examination of Jawhariyyeh's seven photographic albums that affirm the social life and material reality of Palestinians inevitably interrupts and denaturalizes the logic of Zionist settler colonialism. *Camera Palæstina*, then, hopes to contribute to the body of scholarship that witnesses the history of Palestine that settler-colonial ideology, economy, and state power relentlessly work to erase. In this regard, our engagement with Jawhariyyeh is both an "archaeology of [indigenous] knowledge" and an exercise in Arab knowledge-production whereby we three scholars engage with the empirical and social ways the living history of Arab Palestine intersects, informs, and emerges in the living present of Palestine. We, therefore, explore a historical Palestinian visuality, identifying that it is inextricably entangled within a hegemonic Orientalist, Zionist, and colonialist visuality. But also, like Arab modernity itself, we mark Palestinian presence in the construction of this visuality and amplify how that presence grows from and is riveted to Palestine, historically, geographically, socially, and culturally.

We, as authors of this book, have three different disciplinary backgrounds. Our friendship and collaboration came together precisely because of our shared interest in and affection for photography, Wasif, and Palestine. Each of us approach the Jawhariyyeh albums from different perspectives: cultural, political, and social history. Our contributions offer varying, albeit not conflicting, readings of Jawhariyyeh's albums. We offer three intertwined perspectives on the position of these albums vis-à-vis the social and political life of late Ottoman Palestine, without assuaging, displacing, or glossing over the antagonistic and agonistic difference(s) within that very counter-history we seek to highlight. Indeed, Jawhariyyeh's albums are eclectic. The diversity of methodologies and disciplines that we offer in this book uniquely equips us to creatively approach Wasif's multifaceted albums through a number of different disciplinary lenses, namely through the study of photography, history, and historical sociology. Jawhariyyeh's oeuvre, in fact, demands such an approach, channeling us to deliberate the overlay and relationship between history, space, politics, written narrative, and photography.

The challenge in writing this book, therefore, lies not in disputing the framing, the organization, or the representational register of photographs cast by hegemonic narratives, whether they be nationalist, Orientalist, or Zionist. We are not overly concerned with whether or not a character-type of a coffee-seller or shoemaker is true or false, or even if Jawhayyireh exaggerates or downplays a particular event or personality. Nor do we consider the mass of images to offer a definitive social history of twentieth-century Palestine or a comprehensive knowledge of social use of photography in the Arab world before World War II. However, if we are not offering a comprehensive history of the Mandate or photography, we do actively seek to locate contexts: of Arab modernity in Palestine, political activism and aspirations of independence during the British mandate, of social relations within Jerusalem (al-Quds) and Palestine (Falastin) in the wake of the Ottoman Empire and rise of new sorts of ruling classes, and, of course, of Zionist settler colonialism which foreshadowed mass, organized, and calculated Zionist violence against the Palestinian people that would result in their dispossession. Considering these multiple, coinciding contexts, the challenge in reading these images, individually, and these albums, collectively, arises from all the ways the images and albums communicate. To whom are they speaking, and how do they communicate to us within their multiple contexts? What is the discursive, class, gendered, and political work that each of these photographs do, individually and collectively as albums?

It is in the living cross-section of these contexts that the photography exists and that we find what we might call the "Palestinian spectator," or, more simply, the Palestinian agentic subject. This subject or "spectator," we will show, is not a passive Palestinian onlooker, a lost subject of the past, or a unified nationalist and historical (male) actor. Indeed, our critical approach to this collection is that the Palestinian subject of photography is far too often represented as passive and one-dimensional, with few exceptions. Indeed, it is not coincidental that among those exceptions are the images produced by photography units of the PLO and PFLP, who portrayed Palestinians (*fida'iyin*, fellahin, and refugees alike) as actively maintaining Palestinian identity along with a claim to all of historic Palestine.[2]

In other words, the starting point for this study is rejecting a nostalgic framework that erases social relations within the Palestinian polity and sees Palestinians in photographs as one-dimensional, frozen, lost, and tragic objects of the past. On the contrary, we see in the active presence of Palestinian subjects in the photographs the precedent to the counter-visuality offered by the Palestinian Resistance. To understand the Palestinians themselves as subjects of their own visual field is to see an *indigenous* visual understanding (or visuality) that stands opposed to dominant hegemonic regimes, whether they be Orientalist, British colonialist, or Zionist settler colonialist, that negate their presence physically, historically, and visually. To be clear, Palestinians always simultaneously co-existed, contested, and, at times, collaborated with those colonial regimes and visualities. What we are saying, however, is that they did so as visual, willful subjects, who populated and belonged to the Palestine.

We approach Jawhariyyeh's seven albums as a rare opportunity. They provide us with a chance to collaboratively examine an indigenously-composed visual compendium to Palestine during the late Ottoman and Mandate period. It is a visual compendium composed as a documentary project and a self-consciously—and at times, self-reflective—historical project. Therefore, we have an opportunity to encounter a Palestinian spectator. It may be rightly observed that Jawhariyyeh's images of the "Palestinian" was saturated with his own class, gendered, and geographic prejudices and assumptions. Compressing Jawhariyyeh's prejudices into a national subject, however, may be productive in revealing a composite of the "Palestinian spectator," who functions as a compendium of a number of subject positions (male, female, peasant, bourgeois, Christian, Muslim, etc.) just as these albums themselves are multifaceted, allowing many competing subjectivities to emerge. Despite the differences in our own approaches, in our journey through Jawhariyyeh's albums each of us encountered the Palestinian as an active and mindful national, class, and gendered subject or "spectator," not as a displaced subject of history whose relationship to the photograph is one of nostalgia and passivity. We found a complex transhistorical subject, who cohabitates temporalities of a regime of visuality (now and then) that understands Palestine not as a historical bygone but *as a lived and living social fact.* More simply put, this book offers a *popular* history of the Palestinian subject, of Palestinian photography, and of Mandate Palestine (especially centered around its historical capital, Jerusalem) as emerging through the visual archive that connects them. It is a popular history that writes Palestinians back into the history of both Palestine and the photography of it.

A BRIEF HISTORY: INDIGENOUS PHOTOGRAPHY IN PALESTINE

Currently, an emerging history of photography in Southwest Asia is freeing us from the hegemony of a Eurocentric history of photography, one that sees indigenous production only through the prism of mimicry. Recent scholarship is provincializing European photography and dispelling the conception of photographic practice as a European import and, therefore, indigenous and foreign photographies as two discrete practices.[3] Therefore, this study first acknowledges that photography as a medium of Jawhariyyeh's history-telling must be understood within the context of the history of photography in the Arab world and within the context of the late Ottoman period and *al-nahdah al-'arabiyah* (the Arab Renaissance).[4]

Within a short period after its "invention" in 1839, the Ottoman court adopted photography and it is said to have been practiced by Sultans Abdülmacid and Abdülaziz. The Abdullah Frères and Pascal Sébah (and eventually his son Jean) would become the Ottoman Middle East's most renowned photographers, far surpassing any European photographer in prestige and output, if not quality. Less well-known is that, in 1861, Muhammad Said Pasha, the Wali of Egypt, sent the first photographer and cartographer, Muhammad Sadiq Bey, to Medina. Sadiq Bey would be the first to photograph Mecca some years later. By the turn of the century, Armenian and Arab photographers became established in Palestine. It is their production that makes a considerable appearance and imprint within Jawhariyyeh's albums.

When we speak of Arab Palestine, we do not intend to displace, ignore or undervalue the non-Arab population of Palestine, particularly Armenian Palestinians who have been an integral part of Palestinian and non-Palestinian Arab society for centuries. In fact, Palestine's most famous photographer was Garabed Krikorian (1847–1920), an Armenian Jerusalemite. Krikorian was Palestine's most prolific studio photographer. Virtually everyone within Jawhariyyeh's milieu would have had their portrait taken by Krikorian's studio sometime during their lifetime, which would explain the number of Krikorian portraits in the albums. Krikorian was a member of Jerusalem's ancient Armenian community and learned photography from the Armenian patriarch of Jerusalem, Yesayi Garabedian (1825–85), who himself was a photography pioneer in Palestine and the Arab world. Garabedian established Palestine's first native-run *atelier* in Jerusalem's Armenian Monastery of St. James in 1859, where he institutionalized photography as a part of the curriculum.[5] Apart from this accomplishment and writing a number of photography manuals in Armenian, which remain unpublished, he is best remembered for training several generations of leading Armenian photographers, most prominently Krikorian. By the 1880s, Krikorian had a studio outside the Bab al-Khalil, or "Jaffa Gate," near Jerusalem's Central Station, the Hotel Fast, and the Thomas Cooke Travel office, all of which provided him with a thriving business.[6]

Born in Lebanon and having moved to Palestine as a child, Khalil Raad apprenticed with Krikorian. Raad opened a rival studio across the street from his mentor by the 1890s, causing a scandal. After two decades of acrimony, Raad's niece, Najla, married Johannes Krikorian, Garabed's son. The two studios decided to collaborate and share the Palestinian market. The Krikorian studio would produce studio portraiture while the Raad shop focused largely on the tourist market, photographing current events and religious and archeological sites. According to the advertisement on the cover of his 1933 *Catalogue for Lantern Slides and Views*, Raad was the "photographer of sites, scenes, ceremonies, costumes, etc."[7] That said, Krikorian, too, catered to the thirst for biblical and Orientalist imagery, producing countless studio portraits of tourists (and middle- and upper-class Palestinians), who would dress in "native," "traditional," often Bedouin, villager or peasant costume.[8]

Krikorian and Raad were not the only Palestinian photographers. They had contemporaries such as the enigmatic Daoud Saboungi (Sabunji), related to Georges Saboungi, ostensibly the first Arab studio owner in Beirut.[9] Based in Jaffa, Daoud Saboungi's photographs are known particularly because he, along with Raad and the Ottoman Turkish photographer 'Ali Sami Bey, were charged with photographically documenting Kaiser Wilhelm's and his wife Augusta Victoria's visit to Palestine in 1898. Palestinian photographers such as Issa Sawabini also photographed the royal visit. Trained in Russian, Issa Sawabini opened a flourishing Jaffa studio in the 1890s (fig. 1.1).

The American Colony's story is better known, and they are responsible for a large number of iconic images, both of current events and tourist images, of Palestine. It is not coincidental that, among all ateliers and photographers, Jawhariyyeh

FIGURE 1.1. Celebration for the arrival of the Ottoman pilot Nuri Bey Nuri and his co-pilot Isma'il Bey. Their departure from Yaffa was the afternoon of 1 April, 1914. Photographer: Issa Sawabini. Jawhariyyeh Album 1, IPS Beirut.

relies extensively on the American Colony production. The American Colony Photography Department grew out of a messianic colony of American immigrants of Swedish origin, who initially started an atelier as one of a number of means to generate revenue. While Fredrick Vester and John Whiting started it, Elijeh Meyers, an Indian Jewish convert to Protestantism, is known for taking it over and training Lewis Larson and G. Eric Matson, who would run the studio for two decades. Less noted, Palestinians Fareed Naseef (Nasif) and the brothers Jamil and Najib Albina worked in the Photography Department as photographers and what we would call today fixers.[10] Better known is that Hanna Safieh (Safiyah) (1910–79) apprenticed in the American Colony. Like Jawhariyyeh, Safieh also worked in the British Mandate government as a Public Information Officer, or effectively the official photographer for the Mandate administration.[11]

WASIF JAWHARIYYEH'S ALBUMS

The original, handwritten version of the Jawhariyyeh Photographic Collection is located in Athens at the Jawhariyyeh family home. An un-indexed photographic album in the Athens collection also contains a number of personal family photographs and other loose images, many of which are amateur photographs not produced by commercial studios. While we do not know if Wasif himself took some of these photographs, it seems quite certain that he or his family or friends did. A typewritten facsimile of the original albums, a typed index of the reference catalogue, and a handwritten index are archived at the Institute of Palestine Studies (IPS) in Beirut, where the bulk of our research was completed. The Collection is composed of five components: hand-written memoirs in three bound volumes; seven volumes of photographic albums—captioned and numbered; a seventy-eight-page reference catalogue; a fourteen-page index and summary of

FIGURE 1.2. Wasif Jawhariyyeh's Original Index Sample—Volume One of Photographic Album. Jawhariyyeh Collection, IPS Beirut.

the reference catalogue; and, finally, a folder containing un-indexed photographs (in Athens only).

Wasif organized his photographic collection into seven albums containing a total of 890 images taken by well-known Armenian, Arab, and European photographers from the period. The albums were arranged chronologically and thematically—almost exclusively around the people, notables, and landscape of Jerusalem and its vicinity. While including a number of portraits of Ottoman provincial governors, foreign dignitaries, colonial officers and administrators, the first two volumes are largely populated by Palestinian notables, judges, doctors, craftsmen, mayors of the city, doctors, and clerics—the first album devoted to Ottoman Jerusalem and the second to Mandate Jerusalem. The subsequent volumes contain Jerusalem landmarks and buildings, neighborhoods, ceremonial processions and historical events (such as the constitutional revolution demonstrations). Volumes 2 and 3 cover the end of the Ottoman administration and events and people from World War 1. Along with images of army installations, military maneuvers, public hangings, and trench warfare, we meet military commanders, officers, and public personalities from Palestine, Syria and Anatolia. Volumes 3 and 4 contain material on the military administration of Palestine (1918–20), the British Mandate, and begin to witness the mobilization of Palestinians against both British colonialism and Zionist settlement. The last two volumes are largely concerned with representing the Jerusalem cityscape and the landscape around the city itself. All photographs are captioned and frequently marked with numbers corresponding to the names and references to people and places (fig. 1.2).

There are several important differences between the IPS collection (Beirut) and the Athens collection—the most significant being the enhanced clarity of Athens over the Beirut copy. The Athens collection contains numerical entries on the photographs whose identification is available on the back of the glued photographs. Those are not available in Beirut except on the few photographs that are captioned underneath. Additionally, the Athens collection contain a number of family photographs that are missing from the Beirut collection. As we will see, the coherence of these albums comes less from their organization than a reading of this organization.

With that said, Wasif Jawhariyyeh was concerned with making his albums intelligible. He was a man of the people, and photography was a practice with an increasing mass appeal. His subjective imagination and way he saw Jerusalem grew out of a bourgeois national—and particularly a male, "middling"— selfhood, forged during the late Ottoman period, in the company of the empire-wide *effendiyah* class.[12] Sherene Seikaly shows, however, that the "middle class" was not homogenous and had different political convictions and economic interests (for example, the position of merchants and the Palestinian bourgeoisie regarding the revolt and boycott of the 1930s, with its potential to harm the "national" economy).[13] While appreciating the important work that has documented Palestinian nationalism as a project that stretches back well before 1948 (in contrast to Zionist assertions), Seikaly acknowledges the colonial epistemologies of nationalism as an analytic rubric and argues for expanding notions of subjectivity to "move beyond nationalism" to include striations of class (and gender) as constitutive of subjectivity.[14] Squarely rooted in a particular petit-bourgeois functionary sensibility, the collection of photographic albums was fashioned, starting in 1924, by a complex character: an Orthodox Christian petit-bureaucrat, a fixer to his notable clients, an Ottoman citizen, a subject of British rule, a refugee, a Jerusalemite musician, an amateur collector, curator and antiquarian, and, above all, a self-styled local historian. He certainly interacted with the peasant and working classes of Jerusalem and its surroundings as much as he operated within the middle and upper classes of the city. As a collector of photographic images, Wasif's eclectic approach was often influenced by the biblical and Orientalist framing of the very sources for his photography, most prominently photographic craftsmen like Raad, Krikorian, and Lars Larsson from the American Colony. Yet the albums depict the political life and social space of Jerusalem during his lifetime in the city, which ended in 1948. We also discern quite clearly that the organization and layout of the photographs was not haphazard but calculated and thought-through as there are two sets of numbers that organize and then reorganize the order in which the photographs were displayed and, therefore, the visual narrative presented. This book approaches the albums and its photographs on various levels: as a historical narrative; as individual photographs of various subjects; as historical documents on the period; and as sources for the study of the social relations in Palestine at the time.

FROM THE LATE OTTOMAN EMPIRE
TO THE MANDATE

The albums in question have their own history as a collection, not only in the way they were collected, composed, and re-composed, but also in their journey to their final resting place(s) in the Jawhariyyeh family personal collection in Athens and in Beirut at the archive of the Institute for Palestine Studies. Wasif collected the albums starting in 1924, though the first is devoted to an earlier period. The images themselves seemed to be a part of a larger project of gathering artifacts and objects from Palestine and the Arab world that would make up the Jawhariyyeh Collection. The latter included a substantial collection of objets d'art, ouds, and other musical instruments, which he began to display in his house in 1929. In 1948, following events in the neighborhood of the western part of Jerusalem where Wasif lived, the family fled their home, leaving behind, among other things, the albums themselves, carefully hidden behind a wall in the house. Fortunately, these were not discovered by the occupiers and hence escaped the organized looting that was taking place at the time by Zionist troops. The albums were unearthed only in the aftermath of the Israeli occupation of the rest of the city in June 1967. At this time, Wasif provided his brother in-law, a resident of east Jerusalem at the time, with detailed instructions on where to find the albums. It was Wasif's good luck that the house was in the hands of a foreign consulate that allowed the brother in-law to retrieve the albums from where they were hidden.

The albums ended up in Beirut, where Wasif lived in exile. There he was able to revisit them and make a copy of the entire album that he gifted to the Institute for Palestine Studies shortly before his death. One wonders if his desire to make a copy of his collection was a consequence of an anxiety about losing it once again, a fear that was not unfounded considering that the Israeli Army ransacked and appropriated the archives of the IPS during its brutal 1982 invasion. The original albums, along with a number of other images, were kept by Wasif's son, who by then had moved to Athens, Greece.

Wasif himself was born in the last decade of the nineteenth century when Palestine was under the rule of Sultan Abdülhamid II. The thirty-fourth sultan in the long history of the Empire was the longest ruling, as he ascended to the throne in 1876 at the height of the crucial reform period known as the *Tanzimat*. In December of the same year, he addressed the first elected Ottoman Parliament, *Majlis al-Mub'uthan*, which he dissolved shortly thereafter. Abdülhamid's period in power was unstable. The Empire went to war against Russia in 1877; French and British meddling in their foreign and internal affairs were at their height; and liberties and rights in the sultanate were restricted after he suspended the constitution, driving underground Arab, Turkish, and Armenian reformers and nationalists. While these events predated Wasif's life by some decades, their impact resonates beyond his early childhood years in Jerusalem during the tumultuous final decade of

Abdülhamid's reign. Wasif's father, Jeries (Jiris), was a member of the city council and close to the pro-Abdülhamid officials at the time. This may be why Wasif included in his album a portrait of the Sultan, along with a variety of Ottoman officials who governed the district of Jerusalem before his childhood. Coming of age after the Sultan was deposed in 1909, Wasif showed enthusiasm in his memoirs for the revolt of 1908 championed by the Committee of Union and Progress (CUP). In his albums, he included a photograph of the mass public celebration in Jerusalem upon the news of the Young Turk revolt and Abdülhamid's overthrow.

As the Empire entered into the Great War, Wasif and his brother were drafted and assigned to the Ottoman Navy at the Dead Sea. Jerusalem eventually fell to the British in December 1917. The event should not be underplayed. The context of World War 1, however, must not be read through the prism of European history. Forced conscription was imposed on the male population of Palestine, with many recruits being shipped to far-away fronts never to return.[15] The period of the war was also a period of great economic hardships. A great famine resulted from a massive locust invasion in 1915, coupled with the sea embargo imposed on the eastern Mediterranean region by the British and French navies. Statistics suggest that one-fourth to one-fifth of the population of greater Syria perished in this famine.[16]

Strict military rule was imposed on Palestine and the region during the reign of Jamal Pasha, the Ottoman Governor of Syria from 1914 to 1918). The Pasha was a member of the ruling triumvirate that controlled the decision making in the Empire, and was appointed as the commander of the Ottoman Fourth Army in Syria, Lebanon, and Palestine. He is frequently represented in Jawhariyyeh's albums (fig. 1.3). Ottoman provisional law, granted to him in May 1915, endowed him with unprecedented emergency powers, which he was quick to use against the population. His orders to hang a number of Arab nationalist figures in Damascus and Beirut gave him the reputation of "the butcher" or *al-Saffah*. Considering his summary public executions of Arab nationalists and his role in the Armenian Genocide, the title became his nickname among the Arab and Armenian populations of the region.

Aware of the reputation of Jamal Pasha, in the first album Wasif included a photograph of a hanging that took place in Jerusalem. In his memoirs he even used the term *al-Saffah* to refer to the pasha—but not in the albums. Jamal featured in the first album as a grandiose leader with portraits that show him leading the troops. Jawhariyyeh's ambivalence towards the pasha was perhaps symptomatic of the entire population, and of his and his family's relationship with the Ottoman administration. On the one hand, he hated the pasha's rule, which was marked by the coup within the CUP by Enver, Talaat, and Jamal Pashas, who tended towards Turkish nationalism and suppression of Arab, Armenian, and other ethnic-based political movements in the multiethnic Empire. On the other hand, during the war Jawhariyyeh showed a level of patriotism towards the Empire, in

FIGURE 1.3. Jamal Pasha on Horse at the Dead Sea. Jawhariyyeh Album 1, IPS Beirut.

whose military he and his brother served, that was characteristic of the majority of the population.

Moreover, in the political mind of Arab Palestine World War 1 marked, not only the end of the political order of the Ottoman Empire, but also a social order governed by Ottoman modernity. The Great War brought an end to centuries of a political, economic, and cultural order where Palestine was an integral part of a regional home. This region was partitioned off by colonial powers against the will of its people. The rise of colonial borders disrupted the centuries of interconnected cultural, social and economic relations between Palestine, Lebanon, Jordan, and Syria, if not Egypt, Iraq, and, what is now known as eastern Turkey. The collusion of the indigenous ruling classes to regularize this partition in the form of nation-states only perpetuated the mutilation of families, social relations, and economies that bound Arab, Armenian, Kurdish and Turkish communities in Southwest Asia. If the shifts, changes, and disruptions that accompanied World War 1 should not be underestimated, the Sykes-Picot Agreement, itself a product of that war, must be understood as nothing short of a cataclysmic disaster for Palestine as well as the population of Southwest Asia. This cultural, social, and economic fabric is clear in Jawhariyyeh's memoirs and, to a large degree, apparent in his index of this photographic narrative.

By the same account, despite the damage that British rule wrought, Wasif includes a number of important photographs of Jerusalem's life during the war that include British presence. Their appearance speaks to the complex contradictions within the colonial bourgeoisie, their desire for liberation and their resistance to colonization but also their regressive desire to maintain and increase power through collaborating with colonial regimes, as Sherene Seikaly teaches us.[17] Jawhariyyeh and his cohort were not above this. He documents the triumphal arrival of the British. Most notably, he provides a number of images of Allenby's entry into the city as well as the famous American Colony photograph of the surrender of the city, which will be discussed at some length in this book (fig. 1.4). By understanding the transition from Ottoman Palestine to the conquest of Palestine by the British, Wasif's images of British troops marching into Jerusalem's Jaffa Gate or the formal surrender of Jerusalem to the British by Hussein Hashim Husseini take on a significance experienced by Palestinians and Arabs in a unique and powerful way.

The British period is widely illustrated in the albums. Following a similar pattern to the one he used in the first album devoted to the Ottoman period, Wasif included photographs and portraits of various local leaders and British officials. Under British rule, the doors of Palestine were opened up widely for European Jewish immigration associated with the Zionist project. Yet, while representing religious leaders from the Old Yishuv, he includes few if any photographs of Zionist leaders. While the local Jewish community of Jerusalem is featured positively in his description of religious, social and ritual life in Palestine during the Ottoman rule in his memoirs, the photographs related to European Jewish colonizers in the albums are, to a large extent, limited to the settler project, including bombings and destroyed buildings resulting from Zionist violence against Palestinians and the British. A notable exception are the graphic and compassionate photographs documenting the 1929 massacre of the Jewish community of al-Khalil (Hebron),

FIGURE 1.4. British Troops Entering Jerusalem via Bab al-Khalil, 1917. Jawhariyyeh Album 1, IPS Beirut.

a mixed community populated by both pre-Zionist Sephardi Jews from the Old Yishuv and some recent Ashkenazi settlers.

Many of the images found in Jawhariyyeh's albums (but not necessarily his photographic collection in total) can be found in other collections, particularly the American Colony and the Eric and Edith Matson Collection now housed at the Library of Congress. Apart from the considerable attention to political activism by Palestinian society during the Mandate, another significance of the albums lies in how Jawhariyyeh illustrates the very fabric of Palestinian society before 1948 not in order to evoke nostalgia but in order to visualize communities, events, rituals, and celebrations that are indigenous to the land of Palestine. This assertion is evident considering the photographs were largely collected throughout the Mandate period and in no way could Wasif had anticipated the catastrophe imposed upon him and the Palestinian people in 1948 by the Zionists with British quiescence if not active support.[18] Following 1948, photographs in the albums were bound to acquire greater significance and become part of the collective memory of the Palestinians. Rather than thinking about this collective memory through a nostalgic lens, we consider that these photographs constitute a historical archive. Each and every one of them, separately or in conversation with other images in and out of the albums, functions as a living, historical document that informs us about a momentous period in the history of the region writ large.

PHOTOGRAPHY AS TITLE TO PALESTINE

Jawhariyyeh's albums are composed of photographs taken by various native and non-local photographers. As such, each image in the collection has a history of its own outside of the collection. These individual photographs tell a story, not only of a society and a worldview, but also of photography and its development in Palestine. Our book tackles the history of camerawork in Palestine and recognizes the role played by a number of local photographers. Photography had a long history in Palestine, dating to the arrival of the first photographers to the country in the same year in which the announcement of new technology was made, 1839. It quickly developed into a local trade practiced by a number of natives throughout the Ottoman lands, including Palestine. Local photographers such as Khalil Raad, Garabed Krikorian, Issa Sawabini, and Daoud Saboungi captured images of the land and the people, documenting customs, annual celebrations, and historic events as well as serving the thirst for "Holy Land" photographs. In contrast, European photographers focused almost exclusively on this latter market, concentrating mostly on scenes, panoramas, ruins, and buildings in Palestine through the prism of the "Holy Land," rather than as a socially-vibrant, inhabited contemporary space. The only other images Europeans may have produced are ethnographic or official, relating to their own economic, military, and political designs.

The history of photography in Palestine, as well as Palestinian photography, will be discussed throughout this book. For now, we would only like to note that the albums include a number of photographic genres. The composite nature of these albums come together as a singular narrative—a composite of various genres of photography and various types of photographers—that overwrites the power of the photographs taken by Orientalist photographers. Jawhariyyeh literally *authorizes* an indigenous narrative: one that is not exclusionary (that is, East vs. West), but a narrative of Arab modernity that compels us to read the mundane and the extraordinary, the Orientalist and the indigenous, as cogently and materially representing Palestinian reality, history, and visuality (all located within Arab, Armenian and Ottoman contexts).

That Wasif created seven photographic albums using largely commercial photographers' images indicates to us that the images, the narrative, Wasif's intent, and the *effect* need to be "read." If the collection is read as a narrative, one must ask how it unfolds, and why does the "author" choose to the visual progression he did? Indeed, we will see how his written memoirs differ from his visual account. This is not to say they contradict one another. Rather, the narrative seams in his "illustrated history of Palestine" differ completely from his memoirs. This book offers a number of different readings of these albums, but each of us notes the narrative shifts. We do not make these observations to disparage or dismiss the validity of Wasif's narrative. To the contrary, we seize on these seams as productive catalysts for generating knowledge about Palestine that has been displaced by Zionist aggression and settler colonialism.

FIGURE 1.5. Nicola Saig, *Caliph Umar at Jerusalem's Gates*, c. 1920. Courtesy of Shouman Foundation, Darat al-Funun, Amman.

For an example, let us return to the earlier discussion of the contradictions within Wasif as an Ottoman citizen, and later the tensions occasioned by shifting between his Ottoman affinities and being a subject of the British Crown. The first page of the album displays three images: a reproduction of the Ottoman tughra, a famous portrait of reform-minded Sultan Abdulāziz, and an etching of Jerusalemite painter Nicola Saig's "Caliph Umar at Jerusalem's Gates" (c. 1920) (fig. 1.5). We are forced to read these images together. In a handwritten explanation below the etching, Wasif explains how the image represents the legendary moment when Orthodox Patriarch of Jerusalem Sophronius surrendered the city in 637 to the Caliph Umar ibn al-Khattab.[19] Umar, one of the four Rashidun Caliphs, was aware of the sensitivity and value of Jerusalem as a religious city. He therefore granted the city's Christians religious and civil freedoms, in addition to permitting Jews to worship in the city for the first time in five centuries. This painting, placed adjacent to the Ottoman standard and the most renowned reformist Sultan, begs to be read allegorically.[20]

Most obviously, the allegory speaks to the importance of interconfessional unity within the city of Jerusalem and the responsibility of the state to ensure that. "Concord and unity" (*al-ulfah wal-ittihad*) was an Ottoman idiom since the Tanzimat. Not only did it address the aspirations of burgeoning national movements within the Empire, but it also was a central organizing metaphor for governing

Lebanon, especially after the civil unrest and massacres of Arab Christians in Mount Lebanon and Damascus in 1860. Indeed Laura Robson and Michelle Campos, respectively, show us the political importance of stressing secular national identity and inter-confessional fraternity during the Mandate.[21] Such a nationalist discourse arises from the literature of the Nahdah, where the Sultan Abdulāziz figures prominently.[22] When one speaks then of Jawhariyyeh's Ottomanism, one speaks of a robust Arab nationalist discourse that finds representation within Ottomanism itself. Before the Turkish nationalist coup within the ruling committee of the CUP, such cultural nationalism was not inherently antithetical to parliamentary Ottomanism.

Yet, the full allegory might not be understood until one reaches the famous image of the surrender of Jerusalem to the British, which is discussed on a number of occasions in this book. That is, the first page of the albums is a nationalist statement issued after the Balfour Declaration, after the Mandate, and after Zionist colonialization became unambiguous as a European Jewish settler colonial project. The three images together express a national and subjective vision of Palestine, along with particular expectations of how Jerusalem, its citizens, and communities should be governed. Palestinian national identity arose out of the Ottoman Empire and was forged not in response to Zionist settler colonialism but through decades of indigenous Arab political writings and activism and, as Lauren Banko shows us, through British colonial policies that explicitly worked to discriminate against Palestine's native Arab inhabitants and favor Jewish Zionist "citizenship."[23]

We may speculate as to Wasif's intentions when we consider which images he included, where he placed them, and their possible inter-relationships with adjacent images. Despite the considerable written resources he left us, including his memoirs and an index to his albums, the logic and reasoning for his choices are verbally unstated. We therefore are left with the effect of the albums and their material histories (which include the histories of their production and their indexical content). If we combine what we have learned from Banko and Ariella Azoulay, as well as a slew of Arab *nahdah* writers and thinkers, about the political rights of the modern Arab subject, we can understand the photographs in Jawhariyyeh's collection as the notarization of the visual title to the land of Palestine.[24] We can read the photographs, individually and collectively, as a visual docket that "documents" the "contract" of Palestinian citizenship, the legal and historic relationship of the indigenous people of Palestine to their country and their society. Therefore, juxtaposing Saig's painting of Umar entering Jerusalem with Sultan Abdulāziz and the Ottoman Standard attests to the expectation of Palestinian citizenship. The celebration of Palestinians in Jerusalem of the Young Ottoman Revolt, then, is both a claim to citizenship, experienced and promised, but also a demonstration to being deprived of it under the colonial rule of the British.

Beyond its service as a "contract" of Palestinian citizenship, as Azoulay might suggest, we seek also to consider paradigms of sociability (including those other than "citizenship" and "sovereignty") that arise out of political and social discourse at play within the Palestinian Arab polity. In doing so, this book aims to demonstrate that the photographs in Jawhariyyeh's albums, individually and collectively, authorize the propriety of Palestine and Jerusalem as its historic and lived city, not as an exclusive national project but also as a political right that was established in the preceding decades. We may consider this, however, with the understanding that "propriety" and property were also negotiated quite differently in the Arab world before World War 1, and even more so before the modern Ottoman Land Code of 1858, which introduced the equivalent of private property, titles, and deeds (*kawshun/kawashin*). Wasif's compiling of these photographs, not after 1948 but throughout the Mandate itself, clearly authorizes these images—even if they were composed by parasitic Orientalist and expatriate entrepreneurial studios such as the American Colony—as a nontransferable *kawshun* to the historical patrimony of the Palestinians to their land if not national identity.

ALL PHOTOGRAPHY IS COLLECTIVE

Cyrus Schayegh asks why we "study the Mandates through the lens of colonialism rather than decolonization."[25] He reminds us that decolonization, like colonialism, is less an event than a process."[26] Corroborating Banko and Seikaly's studies of Palestine during the Mandate, Schayegh suggest that, rather than an exclusively "state-centered," unilateral, and linear analysis of mandates, we should consider a more dialectical reality where mandate regimes ruled, created policy, and acted in contexts that were equally constructed and defined by "playing the political game" with indigenous elites.[27] How then to think about Wasif Jawhariyyeh's self-appointment as a chronicler of Palestinian political and social life? His intimate ties with, indeed service and indebtedness to, Jerusalem's ruling families, are even more complicated in the context of his friendship with British officials and the government registry when he was working in the Werko Office of land taxation.

It is indisputable that Jawhariyyeh intended to document what he saw as key political activities and historical events during the Mandate. These activities were fundamentally anticolonialist, anti-Zionist, and nationalistic. But they were not also anticapitalist or against the indigenous Palestinian ruling class. Wasif was not a revolutionary, nor was he as much of a full-blown libertine as some like to project onto him. He was, undoubtedly, invested in the political status quo of Palestinian political life, as demonstrated by detailed attention given to photographs of Palestinian political congresses, intersectarian conferences, the meetings of the Arab Higher Committee, and visits by Arab and foreign Muslim dignitaries sympathetic with the Palestinian desire for independence (fig. 1.6). The intensity of

FIGURE 1.6. *General Islamic Congress 1921: The meeting was held at Rawdat al-Maʿarif [Jerusalem], 1931.* Album 2, IPS Beirut.

Jawhariyyeh's photographic albums increase during moments of uprising, protest, revolution, and armed struggle, but always maintain a strong political, social, and economic identification with the ruling Palestinian elites, splicing images of political congresses within images of uprisings and violence.

Keeping this in mind, this book expands on readings, techniques, and strategies of how one considers a decolonial prism to diffract the knot of history, the present, ideology, and the world. In the case of Palestine, Jawhariyyeh's albums are both intentionally and unintentionally political in presenting a particular form of "seeing," of visuality, that was a part of Arab modernity. Therefore, rather than think about decolonization only as a means of countering political action, Aníbal Quijano teaches us that the "coloniality of power" refers to the structures of oppression and inequality (including racial hierarchies) that are rooted in and created by but have outlived colonialism.[28] The coloniality of power in Palestine is threefold. The first layer is ushered in by the coloniality of power as introduced during the late Ottoman period; that is, social structures and worldviews that are based on the inequalities inherent to capitalism and modernity instituted by *indigenous* Arab nobles, bourgeoisie, and intellectuals (including *nahdah* intellectuals). These indigenous elites remained active (and complicit) throughout the Mandate and post-Mandate eras. The second is the coloniality of the British Empire itself and how it interlinks with (albeit asymmetrically) indigenous ruling classes. The third, and least surprising but most immediate, sustained, and destructive, is the coloniality of Zionism considered as a settler colonialist practice and worldview. Within this unequal triumvirate of coloniality, systems of hierarchy have been dialectically constructed. What binds this triple coloniality of power is knowledge production and different modes of extraction of surplus capital (land, labor, and resources), modes of extraction that fall doubly on Palestinian women.

On the most immediate level, Jawhariyyeh's albums are a composite text that visualizes Palestine during its transformation from an Ottoman province through the onset of British colonial rule. We have no pretense about his intent. He was not, by any means, a subversive, radical, or prescient savant, a political activist, or a profound intellectual mind. But nevertheless, Wasif's careful construction of years of photographs he collected into a visual narrative about Palestine is unambiguously an attempt at producing indigenous knowledge about the community in which he lived. This kind of knowledge (and accompanying visual narratives) emerged itself within the coloniality of power of the Palestinian elite, but this knowledge does not exist apart from its relationship to the subaltern strata of Palestinian society that always assert themselves in ways that might not be readily intelligible.

While it would be a mistake to approach Jawhariyyeh's albums as a "family album," Marianne Hirsch does show us, using material from the United States, that family albums have typically supported accepted ideological configurations of the idealized family and society. Family photographic albums demonstrate a "familial gaze" as well as a familial look that accepts others as well as selves into the family's narrative.[29] Hirsch's insights direct us to not only consider the representational and ideological nature not only of Wasif's albums themselves—that is, why they might have been composed. She, and other scholars of photography, would have us seek out the discursive, representational, and visual languages that make them intelligible during the Mandate period when Palestinians were articulating a national identity under the conditions of modernity, capitalist transformations, British colonial rule, and Zionist settler colonialism. Wasif's albums certainly are organized according to a particular sort of "familial gaze," a gaze, in this case, of the Palestinian bureaucratic class, invested in forms of order and capital that may have benefited from, and certainly did not disrupt, the colonial order and its social hierarchies.

Having said all of this, we conclude by saying that we write this book to encourage reflection on Palestinian social history and Palestinian photography beyond the confines of one particular era—beyond, for example, the Mandate—just as Schayegh suggests. Likewise, we anticipate ways in which this study might contribute to more than just our understanding of these albums as an articulation of a particular, rather limited subject position, that is, the middle-class, nationalistic, male, heteronormative eyes of Jawhariyyeh. As the *auteur* of the visual narrative in his albums, Wasif appropriates Orientalist, commercial, and news photographs and arranges them into a chronologically and thematically coherent and, indeed, empirically sound and justifiable narrative. But few of these images "belong" exclusively to him. Considering that a large number of evocative and informative images also exist in his personal collection in Athens, his choice of these images in the composition of the albums incited us also to think beyond Jawhariyyeh himself. In peeling back the triumvirate of coloniality (indigenous modernity, British colonialism, and Zionist settler colonialism) that is intertwined with the deployment of appropriated images, we hope to begin to offer an opportunity to engage disparate but interconnected photographs as a transhistorical space to explore the collective identity of Palestinians in relation to their homeland and Jerusalem, their eternal capital.

The Archival and Narrative Nature of the Photographic Albums of Wasif Jawhariyyeh

Issam Nassar

This chapter, and the entire book, is devoted to the study of the photographic albums fashioned by Wasif Jawhariyyeh as the photographic history of Palestine. Although Jawhariyyeh wrote his memoirs and left us his song book, entitled *al-Safinah al-Jawhariyah*, the albums are seen here as standing on their own as objects, both in themselves and as articles of visual representation of the life and times of Jawhariyyeh in Jerusalem. However, it is important to keep in mind that for Wasif, they were part and parcel of his overall project, which he himself called "the Jawhariyyeh Collection," and which includes the memoirs, the photographs, and the artifacts he collected before he was forced out of his home in the western part of the city after the Zionist conquest of that section in 1948.

The covers of the first of the albums state that the collection was "established" in 1924. However, it is unclear if the reference is for the photographic albums alone or the entire body of materials. Jawhariyyeh's own description of the albums, stated on the cover of each, appears initially to be organized chronologically, with the first album bearing the title of "the Ottoman period in Jerusalem," and the second "the pictorial history of Palestine during the British Mandate period." However, in the later albums Wasif did not keep to his proposed periodization.

The task of analyzing photographic albums is not a straightforward process, but one that depends, to a large extent, on being able to unearth the multiple layers that constitute them. In general terms, photographic albums are multifaceted, by their own nature as artifacts and narratives. One layer relates to them being collections of individual photographs, each with its own history and context. The second relates to the fact that they are books of visual narratives, through which stories are being told by their creator, in this case Jawhariyyeh, who saw them as part of his overall project. The third layer relates to their constituting an archive, by the very fact that they preserve photographs. Similarly, albums are significant in a very personal way to the individuals who created, organized, and preserved them, without minimizing the fact that they are products of the historical context in which they were created.

In what follows, I will examine the various layers that constitute the albums of Jawhariyyeh, including their being archives of images, narratives of a particular historical period, and as a construction of a certain *imaginaire*, as Stephen Sheehi will elaborate in Chapter Five, of social and political life in Palestine, and more specifically in Jerusalem. As the task is enormous, with seven albums constituted of more than nine hundred images, I will focus mostly on the first album in the collection, with occasional references to the second. This more granular process will allow the social history of the images as deployed by Jawhariyyeh to emerge. This social history, of course, is revealed in each photograph, but as the crucial part of this study, I point to the collective gathering of these images by Jawhariyyeh as a means to create an historical archive of the social and political life of the Palestine in which he lived.

THE ALBUMS AS ARCHIVES

Albums can be seen as an archive, in general, due to the fact that they document and preserve artifacts of certain moments that now belong to the realm of history. Jawhariyyeh organized these documents, artifacts, and moments in a particular order, just as archivists might. The Jawhariyyeh albums, I argue, acquire a certain excess level of importance due to the material loss of their original subject, Jerusalem as it was at his time. Images from Palestine before its conquest have become foundational elements within the collectivized nostalgia of the Palestinians. The fact that the albums are semi-chronologically organized and include photographs of leaders, rulers, elites, and locations, gave them the power of a narrative urgently needed in the process of nostalgia construction for dispersed Palestinians longing for the lost homeland.

Archives in themselves, as Jacques Derrida argued, synchronize the principles of time, space, and authority. In fact, the very name archive points etymologically to time, space, and order. As Derrida notes, the *archê*, the name given to the institution of the archive, refers to "beginnings," "origins," and "source of action." The source of the term is *arkheion*, which although it referred initially simply to a "house," became associated with the residence of the superior magistrates, or the archons, who had the power to declare laws.[1] A source of the power of the *arkheion* was the fact that it housed official documents. In this sense, the very idea of the archive from its inception was connected with the exercise of power. At the same time, the *arkheion*, being a house, is a material place that physically exists and has its own address.

The archive as such combines time, space (with the historical, ontological, material), and authority. As collections of artifacts amassed in a certain order to serve a particular power structure, archives represent a vision of the unchallenged truths necessary for those in control. The materials states collect in the archives (for example, records of birth and death and location, criminal proceedings, taxes and licenses) are those important for the way they control society, exercise their authority, and preserve their memory as institutions. Although the collected materials are classified by certain principles of period, location, and institution, the most important principle is often related to the exercise of power and control. States and institutions are not the only authorities that create archives: individuals also make their own archives, synchronizing their own authority over time and space. However, when individuals collect, they often do not use the term archive to describe their collections or even think of them in archival terms. But the dynamics of collecting and ordering do not deviate much from the same principle of the exercise of power, albeit a different kind of power, one that relates to personal needs and desires.

Individuals collect documentary artifacts for various reasons, some of which include the need to preserve official documents necessary to survival in the legal and political structures in which they live, such as birth certificates, old passports, property deeds, educational or professional credentials. Other collections contain artifacts with sentimental value to personal, familial or communal lives. Additionally, individuals construct collections, in many cases, as ways to attest to how they see themselves and their roles in the world around them. Although individual collections are not often of great importance to state authorities, to historians they serve to highlight elements of the past both as practices and as sources for historical documentation. Historians use such materials not only as evidence of events that occurred in the past, but as pathways through which they can construct the *mentalité*, or the worldview, and the historical imagination related to the periods they study.

Wasif fashioned his albums in a way that gave them the aura of officialdom. The first photograph in album no. 1, for example, was supposed to be that of the Ottoman Sultan Abdülhamid II, and the emblem of the Ottoman state. Jawhariyyeh never inserted the photograph, but he did leave a blank space for it. He adorned the notebook that accompanied the album with the emblem and dedicated it to both the Sultan and the governor of Jerusalem (fig. 2.1). The dedication reads as follows:

> I adorn this book with the emblem of the Ottoman state [. . .] his royal majesty Sultan Abdülaziz, one of the great kings of the Ottoman State who was followed in the high position by his brother Sultan Abdülhamid. And with a photo of his Excellency Ra'uf Pasha, the *mutasarrif* of Jerusalem.

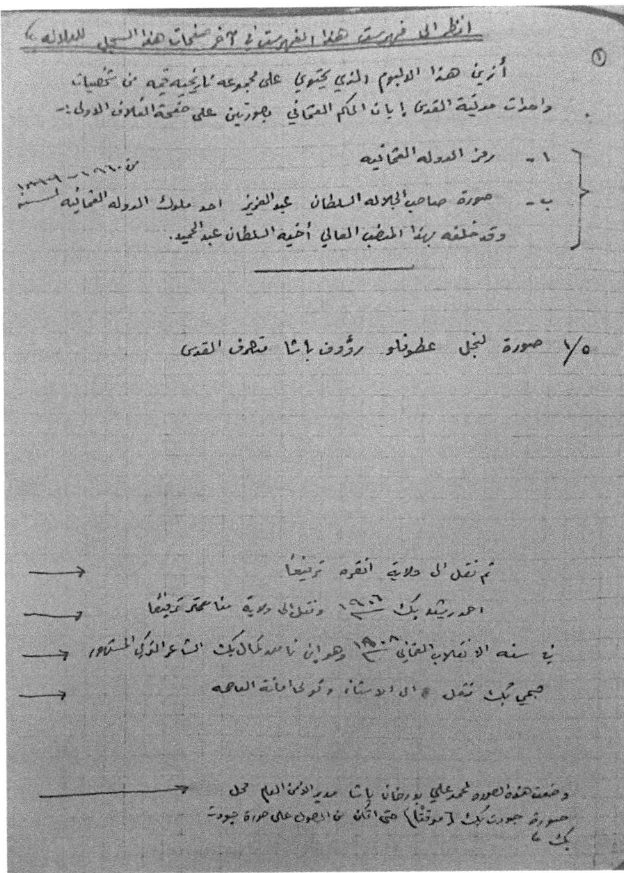

FIGURE 2.1. Jawhariyyeh's description of the inclusion of the photographs of the Sultan. Index to Jawhariyyeh Collection, IPS Beirut.

Interestingly enough, if the album collection started in 1924, as stated above, then this dedication to the sultan would have been meaningless, considering that the sultanate no longer existed and the Sultan himself would have been dead for more than six years. Dedicating a personal collection—an album in this case—to any ruler appears to be an unusual, if not peculiar, act to say the least. More oddly still, the Sultan to whom he dedicated the album had been removed from power in 1909, when Jawhariyyeh himself would have been no more than a teenager. In addition, in his own memoirs Jawhariyyeh showed disapproval, if not outright animosity, towards this specific sultan.

The dedication, then, did not serve Wasif as a means of getting favors from the Ottoman authorities, as was the traditional motivation for the practice. Still, such an act of dedication could serve as an indication of Jawhariyyeh's intention in collecting the photographs and fashioning them into an album. It functions as a means of giving the album an aura of formal legitimacy. By including such a dedication, Wasif intended to give merit to the album as a public work and show-case it as if it was a published book.

The archival nature of the albums is further confirmed by examining the seven albums that were intended to be divided chronologically, starting with the late Ottoman period and ending shortly before the events of 1948, although after the first two albums Jawhariyyeh did not consistently maintain chronological organization. They focus on life in Jerusalem, including the political changes that were taking place at each period. The fact that Jawhariyyeh kept a separate notebook for each of the albums, in which he described every picture included, adds to our knowledge on the period depicted. Therefore, from today's standpoint, the albums put together can be described as records documenting the liminal period separating Ottoman rule in Palestine from the creation of the state of Israel. In this sense, the albums can function as an infusion of memories from a period that predates its owner's departure from Palestine in the aftermath of the *Nakba* of 1948. The events of that year had acquired a special meaning within the collective Palestinian memory, not only as references to the past lost, but also as a defining moment, a great juncture, in the historical narrative of the Palestinians.

THE STRUCTURE AND THE NARRATIVE

The narrative presented via the albums functions on several levels. The first is connected with the choice of photographs to include and the way they are organized in the albums. By ordering the photographs in a certain manner, Jawhariyyeh was telling us a story, a visual one in this case. The second level, the captions he provided each photograph in the album, reveals the significance of the photographed in the eyes of Jawhariyyeh. While the visual in each photograph depicts certain people, places or objects, the captions describe how Wasif understood them. The third level derives from the description and information Wasif gave to each photograph in the accompanying notebooks. And the last is drawn from the photographs in the albums and the memoirs Wasif wrote in which he sometimes refers to some specific photographs.

On the visual level, the photographs narrate a story about Jerusalem in which the nobility and the ruling political and religious elites play a central role. The narrative is internally coherent, presenting Jerusalem as a central city in the Ottoman empire, with rulers who were exceptional, and local notables who were, to some extent, the movers and the shakers in the city's life. Then the narrative moves to focus on the Great War in Palestine, with images of troops marching, leaders posing, and soldiers in the trenches.

However, on the level of the captions, the story narrated becomes a little different. It is a story in which Wasif tells us the meaning for each and every picture, often passing judgment or making observations about the depicted events. The choice of captions is not innocent and reflects Wasif's view, and perhaps his

FIGURE 2.2. Picture with arrow pointing to Wasif Jawhariyyeh's home in the Old City. Jawhariyyeh Album 1, IPS Beirut.

reasoning for the choice, of each photograph. While it is true that photographs document and capture singular events in a purely mechanical fashion through the images they preserve on the tin plate, albumen print, or paper, in themselves, they fail to capture the temporal or the social contexts in which they were produced. Photographers, collectors, and owners, such as Jawhariyyeh in our case, therefore, resorted to the written caption to fill in some of the missing information. Captions, however, as important as they are in providing contextual information, provide only partial rather than total descriptions, and are dependent on the interest and knowledge of their writers. A caption given to a photograph of a holy site in Jerusalem can be as simple as the common name of the building currently there, "The Dome of the Rock," or as ideologically freighted as "the site of Solomon's Temple." Describing what is depicted in the picture as the dome or the site, as in our example, only presents us with fragments of the endless possible captions for the image. We can, in fact, imagine various possible captions for the same photograph: "my visit to Jerusalem on a certain date," or "the photographer Bonfils is trying his new camera," or "a holy Muslim site in Jerusalem."[2] The same could be said of any of the captions in Jawhariyyeh's albums. They function as references to the narrative that he chose to weave, rather than as simply general descriptions of what we observe in the photographs. In his first album, for example, Wasif included a photograph of the Old City of Jerusalem from the north (fig. 2.2). The caption he gave to the picture reads as "al-Saadiyeh (*al-S'adiyah*) neighborhood of

Jerusalem," although this particular neighborhood does not actually appear in the photo, as it is located behind the city wall that we see. Wasif added an arrow to the photo, pointing to the location of his childhood home in the city.

Many examples of such selective captions are found in the albums. One more example is the photograph of the surrender of Jerusalem. Wasif took pains in naming each of the Palestinian individuals in the photograph, and even left an empty space in his notebook for the names he forgot, but at the same time, failed to name the two British officers that appeared next to the mayor and his entourage, or the name of the child present in the picture. This stands in stark contrast with the commonly used captions for this widely known photograph were the names of the two British officers are the only ones mentioned. In a book that was widely read in the West, Bertha Spafford Vester, a member of the American Colony group in Jerusalem, failed to mention a single name when printing this photograph besides those of "Sergeant Hurcomb and Sergeant Sedgewick of the 219th Battalion London Regiment," along with the mayor, who she does not name.[3]

The two different captions reveal two different worldviews, one that placed the natives at center stage, and the other that placed the British in the center. In fact, between the photograph, the caption he gave it in the album, and his written memoirs, we are able to witness a practice of Wasif that is present in all the albums: inserting himself in a picture in which he was not present. In narrating the surrender of the city on December 9, 1917, he pointed out that the surrender flag that appears in the photograph was delivered by him personally "to the person holding it in the photograph."[4] His innovative self-inserting narrative into the historical record is not limited to such passing observations as this about the flag, but goes beyond it in his memoirs in which he presents us with details about his movement on that day. On the morning of the surrender, Jawhariyyeh states that he "went with [his] brother Khalil and some friends to Sheikh Badr [the location where the event took place] and headed for the very site where the mayor of Jerusalem had surrendered the city." He might not have been in the photograph, but he was at the site, even though at a later time. Furthermore, Wasif presents us with an account describing the mood in Jerusalem on that day:

> I remember that day as being one of the happiest for the people. They were dancing on the pavement and congratulating each other. Many young Muslim and Christian Arab men, most of whom had been conscripts in Jerusalem during the Turkish era, had changed their army uniforms into civilian clothes in a ridiculous fashion, fearing that the occupying British army might arrest them in their military uniforms and take them as war prisoners. One would be wearing his military trousers and a pair of wooden clogs, with one of those jackets normally worn over the *qumbaz* and an ancient fez on his head, while another wore a *qumbaz* and a *kalpak*, as he did not have a fez.[5]

In a sense, Wasif Jawhariyyeh takes us, his readers/viewers, on a journey through which we can grasp the general disposition of the people of the city on that day. It is the power of his simultaneous narrative describing the same time of the grand event that made him a witness to the event even if he was not physically present at the specific moment documented in the photograph.

Decisions about which photographs to include in the albums, along with the captions provided and the description in the accompanying notebooks, point to a conscious exercise of power by Wasif. The organization of the albums and the order in which the photographs were displayed is another indication of his mindful exercise of power of authorship. As no solid information was provided regarding the photographers or the context in which the images were produced, the authority and the agency in this case resides with the collector of the images and the creator of the albums, Wasif Jawhariyyeh himself. What mattered to him enough to include in the albums is far more specific than all the pictures that he could have had at his disposal at the time. He chose which ones to include, exactly in the same manner as an archivist would choose what is worth preserving and what is not. His selectivity is not innocent but is a product of how he saw his world and his role in it. He thus exercised the same power as all archivists: to establish the very apparatus of the archive.

JERUSALEM IN THE LATE OTTOMAN PERIOD

As mentioned above, Wasif dedicated his first album on the Ottoman period to both the sultan and to the governor of the Jerusalem district. The choice to dedicate the album to an earlier governor of the city is as peculiar as the choice of sultan. The named governor, Ra'uf Pasha, was in Jerusalem before Wasif came of age, and it would not have been possible for him to remember the governor. It is very likely that Jawhariyyeh was echoing his father's admiration for the specific regime that had been overthrown and replaced by one that was significantly different, and perhaps had elements of an anti-Arab xenophobia much more than its predecessor. His father, Jiris Jawhariyyeh, was a "lawyer in his younger years and stood out as a Christian lawyer at Jerusalem's Muslim sharia law courts"[6] during the period of both Sultan Abdülhamid and governor Ra'uf Pasha—whose picture appeared in the first album (fig. 2.3).

Hence, the dedication could be read in some ways more as honoring his father than as reflecting his own politics, which based on his published memoirs appear to have included opposing the Hamidian regime. Still, there is another possibility that could explain such a dedication: namely that the compiler of the album aimed at reflecting the dominant discourse of the periods he was documenting. A sign of such an act can be seen in the photographs of the other authority figures that he included in his albums. Such figures include Jamal Pasha, the head of the fourth Ottoman army in Palestine during The Great War, who is often referred to in the memoirs as "the butcher," as well as the British governors and High Commissioners, who he also opposed, considering them to be enablers of the Zionist colonization of Palestine.[7]

FIGURE 2.3. Photo of Ra'uf Pasha, the *mutasarrif* of Jerusalem, as it appeared in the first album. Jawhariyyeh Album 1, IPS Beirut.

For the most part, Wasif failed to credit the photographers, or to mention the sources of where and how he came to acquire each of these pictures. Only on a few occasions do we find in the notebooks references to certain photographers, such as the photography department of the American Colony in Jerusalem, which Wasif credited for panoramic photographs like that of the Bazaar in Jaffa, or the general view of Ramlah. Other credits were given to the Beirut-based photographer Bonfils, for an image of Ramlah, or for the photographer Doumiani for pictures of Christian religious festivities in the city. As for the sources of the photographs, Wasif failed to name the individual source for each of the photographs he inserted in his album, but he did mention in the notebooks that accompany the albums how he came to acquire some of the pictures:

> I was able, thanks to God, to collect rare and historical pictures from a number of in-dividuals whose affection I am indebted to, such as Sheikh Khalil al-Khalidi, Ahmad Sameh (Samih) al-Khalidi Ismail Bey al-Husseini, Raghib al-Nashashibi, Bishara Habib, and others. May God rest their souls.

The names above are those of some of the most important notables of Jerusa-lem at the time; mentioning them serves Jawhariyyeh well in placing himself as a member, or at least an acquaintance, of the city's elites. The above note refers to the portrait photographs that he placed at the beginning of the first album, rather than to the rest of the collection, which has more of a public nature with its focus on events, processions, and locations. Photographs of a public nature were per-haps easily accessible through the tourist shops in the city, unlike the individual portraits of the notables and leaders. The mere number of portraits of notables, Ottoman officials, governors, and mayors of the city constitutes an important visual archive, perhaps not available anywhere else. As a member of the Greek Orthodox community with strong ties to Patriarch Damianos, who is mentioned several times in the memoirs, Wasif devoted an entire section in the first album to the Orthodox clergy in the city.[8] The album includes fifteen pictures of the vari-ous priests of the city, as well as a number of pictures of what he described in his notebook as "the Arab men of the Patriarchate of Jerusalem." The section on the Orthodox men and priests comes immediately after the long section on the nota-bles of the city, which includes images of mayors, judges, writers, local members of the Ottoman administration, and others. Although in the second album we find similar photographs of the British administrators of the city, the collection in the first album is very significant as it constitutes an archive not found anywhere else. All of the photographs of the "elites" are studio portraits, which makes the pho-tographed subjects appear at their best, in an authoritative manner befitting how Jawhariyyeh represented them in his diaries.

It is worth pointing out, however, that in the section on the Orthodox priests we find a postmortem photograph of Father Saadeh (S'adah). It is the only postmortem image in the collection, if we do not consider the images of dead

FIGURE 2.4. The procession of the Patriarch leaving the Church of the Holy Sepulcher. Jawhariyyeh Album 1, IPS Beirut.

FIGURE 2.5. Festival of Nabi Musa, 1919. Jawhariyyeh Album 1, IPS Beirut.

soldiers in the second album. Where the dead soldiers were in the theater of battle, Saadeh's photograph constitutes a portrait of a named individual, as it is part of the section of images of the clergy. Perhaps this was the first and last known picture of the priest, and no others were taken in his lifetime. Postmortem photography was common at the time in Palestine and elsewhere, with photos of dead loved ones being taken if there were no photographs of them alive. This particular picture is part of Khalil Raad's collection at the Institute for Palestine Studies in Beirut; however, Wasif failed once again to name either the photographer or his source.

The following section in the album includes photographs of religious processions in Jerusalem (fig. 2.4). This is in line with the descriptions of such festivities that appeared in the published memoirs. But unlike the memoirs, in which the festivities of Jewish, Christian, and Muslim communities are described, the majority of the photos in the albums are of Christian, and particularly Orthodox, processions, although a few images of the Muslim festival of Nabi Musa are included (fig. 2.5). In a sense, Wasif has already set up the stage for his narrative in the first album, set within the realm of official Ottoman Jerusalem. Despite any reservations he came to have about that period, he attempted in his album to present it in a positive light as if it was a project of great success.

FIGURE 2.6. Photo from the visit of the emperor. Jawhariyyeh Album 1, IPS Beirut.

THE VISIT OF EMPEROR WILHELM TO JERUSALEM:

The first album appears to some extent to be chronologically organized, with one major exception: the visit of the German emperor to Palestine. This visit took place in 1898, when Wasif was only a toddler, and he was therefore not an eyewitness, yet he still thought it was a significant enough event to include in the album. There is no doubt that the visit was a major event in the life of Jerusalem, and as such, it is likely that its memories were still reverberating in the city many years later. This was perhaps the first visit by a head of state to Jerusalem since the days of the crusades. Royals visited the city in the nineteenth century; Prince Edward (later to be King Edward VII) traveled to Palestine in 1862, and the photographer Francis Bedford accompanied the prince to document the trip, but this was not an official state visit like Wilhelm II's. Wilhelm's arrival brought jubilation to the city, and to a number of Ottoman officials as well as German. It was heavily photographed and the images were used for many years in the commercial advertising of the various photographers who were competing over the title of "official photographer of the emperor" (fig. 2.6). The American Colony photo department made that claim, and so did Garabed Krikorian and Khalil Raad. One would imagine, then, that each sold pictures of the event. If Wasif was collecting his photographs from the local market, then photos of the visit would have been easily accessible. Interestingly enough, the visit is recorded in Wasif's memoirs, despite the lack of any reference to himself or to his family—a trope that is common in the memoirs.

THE GREAT WAR IN PALESTINE

While the first half of the album illustrates the city's rulers and other significant people in power, the second half of the album is devoted to The Great War in Palestine (1914–18), with a large number of photographs that include, but are not limited to, many Ottoman officers and leaders. This section of the album appears to be chronologically organized as well as carefully planned. With a number of images, including a portrait, of Jamal Pasha, the leader of the Fourth Ottoman Army in Syria, then moving on to the "celebrations" held in support of the war effort, the album chronicles the activities of the soldiers in trenches pointing their guns, and medical staff posing for the camera. Together, the pictures in the album appear to be an official narrative presenting leaders, a jubilant population, the marching of soldiers, and medics at work on the front as if this were a story of success.

Most of the images can be traced to two photographic collections, those of John Whiting of the American Colony Photo Department, and the Arab photographer Khalil Raad. Both of those photographers were employed at points to document the Ottoman war efforts in southern Palestine and the Sinai Peninsula. Like elsewhere, Jawhariyyeh failed to credit the photographers, which could be taken as an indication of his disinterest in the pictures in themselves as artifacts, as opposed to his interest in the photographed individuals and groups. It is very likely in this case that the images were bought by Wasif directly from the shops of both near Jerusalem's Bab al-Khalil.

Wasif frames the war in terms of official Ottoman activities, and takes a celebrative tone for the most part. Much of the section on the war includes photographs illustrating the lives of Ottoman soldiers at various locations. Wasif himself was conscripted into the Ottoman navy in the Dead Sea, but the album lacks any images of him or of the specific location where he served.

But one image is more ambiguous; Wasif interrupts the official narrative by including a picture of the hanging of a war deserter (fig. 2.7). This photo is one of only a handful of wartime Jerusalem. The hanging took place outside of the Bab al-Khalil of the Old City of Jerusalem, and was photographed by Khalil Raad, whose studio was located across the street from the execution site. Wasif captioned it, "that is how people were hanged on the gallows—at the Bab al-Khalil square—during the reign of Jamal Pasha, 'the Butcher.'" This caption represents the only time Wasif appears to be critical of the Pasha who is present so often in the album, the memoirs, and the notebooks. Wasif further elaborates on this photograph in his notebook, stating that the hanged man was a member of the navy, and providing the names of the Ottoman soldiers present in a matter-of-fact tone, even mentioning their military ranks. Jamal Pasha appears in several photographs in this section, always looking his best with an aura of authority, not as the ruthless commander who is remembered in Greater Syria (Bilad al-Sham), as well as in the memoirs of Jawhariyyeh himself, as "*al-Safah*," the "blood-shedder," usually translated as "the Butcher."

FIGURE 2.7. Picture of a public hanging. (See Figure 4.3) Jawhariyyeh Album 1, IPS Beirut.

THE ARRIVAL OF THE FIRST PLANE

A rare photograph of the landing of the first Ottoman plane in Palestine is included among the first photographs of the war (fig. 2.8). The plane, according to the caption, arrived in 1914 in Jaffa, but crashed near *Tabariyah* (Tiberias) in the north. Wasif provides the name of the captain and his assistant and informs us that their death was a great tragedy in the "Ottoman kingdom." The photograph is not signed by its maker, and Wasif does not give any information on it. Without the exact date, we cannot be certain whether this was actually the very first plane to land in Palestine or not. There is another photograph in the collection of the American Colony, dated April 1, 1914, of an Ottoman plane with its captain standing in front. This photo's caption states that it is the first plane to land in Jerusalem, with no mention of the fate of the plane or its pilots. Considering that the date of this photograph is April 1st, four months before the Ottomans entered The Great War, and three before the war started, it is very likely that Jawhariyyeh was confused about the arrival of the "first plane." In his diary, he writes that the plane arrived after the war started, and that it did not make it to Jerusalem before it crashed.

Still, the photograph of the Ottoman plane constitutes an important visual reminder of the existence of Ottoman aviation. Shortly before the Ottomans' entry into the Great War, the empire had five aircraft and six pilots, which might explain why the death of two of them was mourned widely in the sultanate, as Jawhariyyeh informs us.[9] While Wasif notes that the plane never arrived in Jerusalem, in his

FIGURE 2.8. Arrival of a Turkish (Ottoman) military plane at Yaffa under the leadership of the officer Nuri Bey, accompanied by his co-pilot Isma'il Bey, 1914. Jawhariyyeh Album 1, IPS Beirut.

memoirs he still describes the pilot, Nuri, as if he had known him well, calling him "one of the best-educated young pilots." The crash of the plane was so grave that, Jawhariyyeh writes, "a special song was composed and sung all over the country to commemorate their deaths, which were seen as a bad omen."[10]

WAR PROPAGANDA

Several photographs in the album were devoted to soldiers and to their military activities, which could be seen as tools of Ottoman propaganda. Among the latter category, we can include the photograph that shows a motorboat in Jerusalem being transported from Jaffa to the Dead Sea, dragged by horses. The photograph is from the collection of John Whiting and appears in the American Colony albums that were dedicated to him. The caption in the Whiting collection dates the photograph to the year 1917. Wasif's description of this photograph in the notebooks provides us with more details about the image:

> A photograph of the first motor boat that the Turkish army brought into Jerusalem on the street outside of the headquarters that used to be Notre Dame. The building was taken over and made into the headquarters of the army inspector, whose name is 'AliRushan Bey, who appears standing on the boat with Nihad Bey, his assistant, next to him. The boat was a gift to an assistant to the late Hussein Hashim al-Husseini towards the end of the war due to his service in erecting the first port on the Dead Sea [. . .] with the aim to transport grains from East Jordan.

While the caption of the original photographer was plain and formal, Wasif's caption not only points out the two important individuals in the picture, but explains the significance of the boat in relation to the economic situation at the time. A sea embargo by the British and French fleets on the shores of the Mediterranean had stopped the imports to Palestine arriving from Europe or Turkey, and Jordan, perhaps due to its proximity to the plains of Hawran in southern Syria, was the main source of grains coming into Palestine.

Among the themes covered in the photographs in this section are soldiers, or officers, standing in individual or group portraits in front of official buildings or their encampments. We also find a few images of troops in the trenches on their stomachs, pointing their guns at what seem to be enemy positions. Those photographs, also from the Whiting albums, appear to be staged. While soldiers are keeping low in the trenches, possibly in order to suggest that they were trying to avoid enemy fire, the angle at which the photos were taken suggests that the camera was placed on a higher level, with its operator standing in full view. If enemy fire was a concern, then a photographer standing in clear view outside the trenches would have been in grave danger. The soldiers are organized in lines, and the fact that they all appear in positions that do not block other soldiers is another indication that the pictures were taken with plenty of time to arrange their subjects, during non-combat moments. The smiling faces or relaxed postures of some of the soldiers also suggest that the kind of stress associated with battle is actually absent.

Still, the careful planning of the images does not make them "fake" or unworthy of our consideration. To start with, they are pictures taken on location, not in a studio, and the individuals appearing in them are genuine soldiers who were stationed at the particular photographed places. Their military status is apparent; the weapons they hold are the ones they used in combat; and the trenches were indeed dug in anticipation of battle. Other photographs, which show troops in military formations or marching through Jerusalem or other locations, do not suggest any form of staging beyond the choice of vantage point and timing.

A number of pictures depict leaders and officers during their visits to Palestine or to the front. Photographs of the visit of Enver Pasha (the Ottoman Minister of War) to Jerusalem accompanied by Jamal Pasha (fig. 2.9) or poses by famous doctors (such as Dr. Tawfiq Canaan), other officers (such as the Mersinli Jamal Pasha), Governor Zaki Bey or Nashat Bey, are informative about the war effort as well as significant regarding the careers of the photographed individuals.

Despite a few pictures in which wounded soldiers display their injuries to the camera, the core of the collection in the album illustrates great organization and readiness for the war (fig. 2.10). The album, then, is more of a piece of visual propaganda than a rigorous coverage of the war and its high cost. The photographs are organized in a "patriotic" fashion that presents a rather heroic narrative. What is clear is that Jawhariyyeh fashioned his albums as a historical record of the times—and of his making of them—more than as a reflection of his personal

FIGURE 2.9. Photo of Enver Pasha at al-Haram al-Sharif, Jerusalem. Jawhariyyeh Album 1, IPS Beirut.

FIGURE 2.10. Distribution of food to Ottoman troops in Palestine. Jawhariyyeh Album 2, IPS Beirut.

feelings or the ties he might have had with the leaders whose photographs adorned his albums. His album of the Ottoman period ends with a famous photograph showing the surrender of Jerusalem to the British forces on December 9, 1917, in which the mayor of the city and his entourage posed with a white flag next to the two soldiers that they encountered on that day (fig. 2.11).

FIGURE 2.11. Mayor's entourage upon surrendering Jerusalem, December 1917. Album 2, IPS Beirut.

Taken by Lars Larson, a photographer from the American Colony group in Jerusalem, this rather famous image had already appeared in numerous publications, with various captions usually highlighting the names of the two British officers. It constitutes a fortuitous example of simultaneous, non-intersecting histories in which the people of the city are often left out. Not only does Jawhariyyeh fail to mention the names of the two officers and instead list the names of everyone else present, but he describes in his caption where he himself was at the time of the event despite his not being in the photograph, or even in the vicinity of the location on which it was shot. By inserting himself into the story, Jawhariyyeh was, in fact, exercising his authority as an archivist and a narrator in the exact fashion discussed above. In his memoirs, Wasif wrote:

> On this day, my brother Khalil, my mother, my brother Fakhri, and I were at my sister 'Afifah's home on the western side of Saint Julian Street. I recall that on that day all Christian denominations rang their church bells to celebrate this happy occasion and held services in their churches. After Hussein Bey al-Husseini officially surrendered the city, the American Colony in Jerusalem published a photograph of historic value, which I have kept in the Jawhariyyeh Collection.[11]

Although Jawhariyyeh was not part of the event, he frames its history, as stated above, not in the context of war, or any other events in Palestine, but in relation to what he was doing. In doing so, Jawhariyyeh deviated from the use of linear time, to the use of what Walter Benjamin called "homogenous, empty time." As Benedict Anderson explained, in this kind of time "simultaneity is . . . transverse, cross-time, marked . . . by "temporal coincidence, and measured by clock and calendar."[12] Wasif inserted himself in the history of a moment with great significance through exercising the power to fashion time and place such that the surrender of the city took place when he was visiting his sister, rather than "when the British won the battle" or "when the Ottomans withdrew," or any other time that would have been possible as a reference.

THE FIRST DECADE OF BRITISH RULE IN PALESTINE

The second album is entitled "The Pictorial History of Palestine During the British Period." The very first photograph in this album is that of the surrender of Jerusalem, mentioned above. Wasif, in other words, chose to both end the first album and start the second one with this photograph, bridging both albums together.

The first group of images in the second album is devoted to the surrender of the city and the entry of General Edmund Allenby two days later—December 11, 1917. Several of the photographs that follow are of dead Ottoman soldiers being buried by the British. Jawhariyyeh also includes a few pictures of meetings between British officials and local Palestinian leaders. However, the most interesting section, in my view, is the one devoted to the bloody events of 1929, when riots and clashes between Jews and Muslims broke out at the Wailing Wall. Wasif's album includes several pictures of the riots in Jerusalem, as well as pictures of Palestinian women demonstrating in protest. We cannot be certain, of course, but this protest could be the very first public action by women in Palestine. The photographs are rare and it is not clear what Wasif's sources for them were, as they are not present in any of the known collections of photographers from that period.

The clashes spread to the nearby city of Hebron, where a massacre of Jewish residents took place. The albums document the aftermath of the massacre (fig. 2.12). This is an interesting addition that further enhances the significance of the collection, as Wasif documents the loss of Jewish life at the hands of his fellow Palestinian Arabs. Still, in his memoirs Jawhariyyeh decries the Zionist faction of Jabotinsky as responsible for the riots that lead to the massacres: "The Revisionist Zionist Party, led by Vladimir Jabotinsky, began to actively call Jews to arm and resort to force, and publicly demanded the takeover of the Wailing Wall in al-Buraq."[13]

Other important photographs in the second album are devoted to the visits of Egyptian, Syrian, and Lebanese artists, singers, and musicians to Jerusalem. We find pictures of famous artists such as the dancers Tahia Carioca (Tahiyah

FIGURE 2.12. Page from the album showing the destruction of Jewish homes in Hebron and Jerusalem, 1929. Jawhariyyeh Album 2, IPS Beirut.

Kariyuka) and Badi'a Masabni, singers Farid al-Atrash and Amin Hassanayn, violin player Sami al-Shawa, comedian 'Ali al-Kassar, and composer 'Umar al-Batsh, among others.[14] While some of these pictures are portraits of the type usually given to fans by artists, other are from Jerusalem, showing the visitors with their hosts from the city. In some instances, a written dedication to Wasif appears on the pictures—as in the case of Sami al-Shawa, who according to Wasif became a close friend and a frequent visitor to Jerusalem. Shawa became "like a member of the Jawhariyyeh family," Wasif wrote in his memoir; "whenever he was in Jerusalem, he would stay with us, as though he was one of us."[15] The frequent appearance of those artists in Wasif's memoirs attests to the extensive web of his relationships to Arab artists from Aleppo, Damascus, Beirut, Alexandria, and Cairo who visited Palestine in the late Ottoman and Mandate periods, but also to the rich network of musicians, singers, artists, and performers that enriched the Palestinian cultural scene in that period.

Strangely enough, these photographs, although grouped together sometimes, are organized more chronologically than thematically. For instance, we find the photograph of the visit of 'Ali al-Kassar (fig. 2.13) appearing on the same page in the album with three other pictures. The first documents the ceremony for the opening of the Jerusalem branch of the YMCA, dated by Wasif as 1932. The second is of the visit of the Indian Muslim leader Mohammad 'Ali Jawhar, referred to by

FIGURE 2.13. The visit of 'Ali al-Kassar to Jerusalem. Jawhariyyeh Album 5, IPS Beirut.

Wasif as Mohammad 'Ali al-Hindi (of India).[16] And the third is of installing electric power in the Christian Quarter of the Old City, also dated 1932. If Jawhariyyeh was attempting to organize the album chronologically, then the mix of themes—which did not occur in the first album on the Ottoman period—would make some sense. Still, the fact that he dated the visit of al-Kassar to 1934, then placed the photograph before the three others from 1932, indicates that Wasif was not always meticulous or careful about the organization of the pictures.

Another important collection of photographs in the album devoted to the Mandate period documents the meetings, conferences, and activities of the Palestine Arab leadership in the city. However, this chapter will not discuss this topic, which I believe requires an entire publication.

IN CONCLUSION

The questions that this chapter set out to tackle relate to understanding albums as archives, as documentary evidence, and to how the Jawhariyyeh album collection functions as a narrative. Several suppositions have emerged to help us answer these questions. The first is the archival nature of the albums. It is clear from examining the Jawhariyyeh albums that they are an archive on their own, as well as in connection to his entire body of work. The photographs are important, each on its own terms, and as a collection. Each of the photographs included, perhaps with no more than a handful of exceptions, depicts a certain individual, event, or place that is of significance to the period. They were organized and categorized by theme and date, although sometimes more rigorously than others. They include captions that describe them, as well as longer descriptions and comments in the notebooks. As in non-personal archives, the photographs are taken out of their original condition as intimate objects and turned into documentary evidence for a period or a theme.

The photographs in the Jawhariyyeh albums are documentary visual evidence for a past that has faded in contrast to seminal events that followed the destruction of Palestine in 1948. As visual documents they have the power to take their viewers on a journey through late Ottoman and British Mandate Palestine. At the same time, they depict significant subjects and construct a visual aura of the periods they depict. As a narrative, the albums recount important elements of the modern history of Palestine, more specifically Jerusalem. The narration starts with photographs of the elites, and moves on to describe the visit of an emperor before delving into festivities and celebrations. It documents change in the infrastructure of Jerusalem—such as the arrival of electricity—as well as the changing landscape of the city. Wasif devoted a long section to the Great War, in which the viewer is introduced to the leaders of the army, the soldiers at the front lines, and is led towards the eventual surrender of the city to the British.

The second album continues the narration with similar tropes: photos of the powerful in the city, including the British leaders. Another element of the narrative that stands out in the second album, and in the other five albums which this chapter has not described, is the photographs of celebrity artists who visited Palestine. The shift in the narrative in this section is interesting, as Wasif takes us spectators into important elements of the social and cultural history of modern Palestine. The fact that he sometimes inserts a photograph of a famous artist on a page that includes other themes integrates the two events together. In this way, Wasif was not just narrating the history of musical performances in Palestine, but incorporating it within the context of the historical transformations that were taking place. As is evident in Wasif's written memoirs, he was a skillful narrator and storyteller. The way his albums are organized further confirms his mastery of narration.

The second album moves on to document grave events through more general images that show crowds, not notables as in the first album. The narrative presented in this section is more nationalistic in nature, even though on at least one occasion it documents the tragedy from the other side of the conflict by devoting a section to the massacre of the Jews of Hebron in a sympathetic tone. Was Wasif concerned about the fate of the Palestinian Jews at this time of intense Zionist colonization? Did he think of them as part of the Palestinian community that fell victim to the unfolding events? While we cannot be certain, the memoirs offer us a clue, for those devoted to the Ottoman and early British periods indicate that among his social milieu were a number of Palestinian Jews. His description of Jewish festivities in the city, and of his performing on such occasions, is a clear indication of how the Jews of Palestine were seen as natives, unlike the Zionist immigrants. The albums in general illustrate life as it was seen and experienced by Wasif, the native son of Jerusalem. They represent life in the city before Palestine was colonized and, in its place, Israel was created. An important element of the Zionist conquest of Palestine has been the erasure of any memory of religious coexistence, a fact that the albums dispute.

In the words of the teacher of Saeed (Sa'id) in Emile Habibi's *The Pessoptimist*, "Conquerors, my son, consider as true history only what they have themselves fabricated."[17] Wasif managed in his albums, as well as his entire project, to preserve a memory of an alternative history of Palestine, one that is not fabricated by the conquerors. In doing so, Wasif wove his visual history in the form of a story in which events were not chronicled as a dry historical account, but rather as a personalized story in which he emerged as its protagonist. The most remarkable side of his visual narrative, in my view, resides in his ability to insert himself into the pictures even when he is not present in them. While in his written memoirs Wasif was at the center of events, as a witness to what was taking place around him, in his albums he inserted himself through the captions and the comments he recorded in the notebooks that he left alongside the albums.

Jawhariyyeh was not a national or renowned figure—or as he puts it in the very first line of his memoirs, "I am no skilled writer, famous historian, or experienced traveler." However, he insisted through his narrative, both the written and the visual, that he was an actor in the play that was being improvised all around him. Perhaps the best description that could be applied to him comes again from Habibi:

> You said you never noticed me before. That's because you lack sensitivity, my good friend. How very often you have seen my name in the leading newspapers . . . [they publish] the names of everyone notable . . . but merely [give] general reference to the rest. The rest—yes that's me![18]

Habibi's Saeed was a version of Voltaire's Candide, while Wasif's persona is more of the storyteller. However, like Saeed, Wasif was keen to mention that he often was in the company of local leaders, mayors, military officials, and renowned artists visiting Palestine. While there is little reason to doubt these accounts of being in the company of the famous, there is no concrete way to verify their truthfulness. Still, even without solid evidence, the narrations of the gatherings, and the events that he witnessed, are of great importance, as they allow us to imagine the time period and the events unfolding. Wasif might not have been the center of the events he recounts in his memoirs, but he certainly appears to be a witness who was present, whether directly or indirectly, at the time of the occurrences.[19]

Like his memoirs, Wasif Jawhariyyeh's seven albums function as bearers of memory, as well as testimonials for a time that has ceased to exist. They document a life bygone that spanned a period close to five decades, during which Jerusalem and Palestine changed hands from a large Ottoman Empire to a much smaller entity ruled by the even larger British colonial empire. This time witnessed the start of Jewish Zionist immigration to the country and ended with the complete disappearance of Palestine from the map of the region.

Jawhariyyeh, himself, was an eyewitness to an era that spanned the last decade of Ottoman rule over Palestine and the entire British Mandate period. His albums are organized chronologically, with the first devoted to the Ottoman period and the second to the British Mandate period. Still, the chronological order was disrupted in the rest of the albums, though they all were devoted to the British period. His memoirs narrate a history from the margins—not to be confused with the history of the margin. While the historical record might present a grand event in its relation to the linear history of the time, such as the surrender of Jerusalem to the British in 1917, Wasif's account presents us with the unexpected, in the sense that it details what he did on that day and how he felt about the surrender. His memoirs constitute a historical narrative from within, rather than from outside, and his careful photographic documentation of the event, along with the details he provided in the accompanying notebooks, function in the same manner.

3

Visual Interlude

Photographic Images
from Ottoman and Mandate Palestine

The selection of photographs in this section come from the albums of Wasif Jawhariyyeh that are in discussion in this book. While we are mindful that they are only a small fraction of the images, we present them in order to illustrate a number of different dimensions of the visual narrative that Jawhariyyeh unfolds for his viewership. Few images in his albums are self-generated, and none of the photographs in this *Visual Interlude* were taken by him personally, although he appears in one (see fig. 3.17). These images represent the photographs that he collected through different means, over different periods in his life, and ones he valued enough to carefully place within the narrative of his albums. Many of these images are easily found, especially those produced by the American Colony's Department of Photography, which can all be located in the Library of Congress in Washington, DC. Yet, for us, the value of the images lies not in their "originality" but in the ways they are located in relation to one another and in relation to the historical experiences that Jawhariyyeh was registering. Moreover, the value and coherence of the images emerge from meaning produced precisely through their deployment within a visual compendium of an "illustrated history of Palestine."

We also need to recognize that the *Visual Interlude* makes stark the gender imbalance in Jawhariyyeh's albums and, therefore, in his visual narrative. It is true that women have a considerably more prominent place, even if they are still underrepresented, in his written narrative. Images of women are found throughout the seven albums. The largest cluster of named, known women is the intervention by Arab Women's Executive Committee (see chapter 5 and fig. 3.1). Women are often named as members of families, described in relation to their male counterparts (as wives, sisters, aunts, etc.), and in relation to their social networks, geographies, and communities. Palestinian women appear often in family, school, and institutional

45

group portraits. But more often than not, their appearance is linked to their class privilege and their relationship to the new effendi, emergent bourgeoisie, and/or elite ʿayan families. Portraits of non-Arab and non-Palestinian women (particularly women related to colonial authorities) and even character portraits of Arab women (see fig. 3.20) appear infrequently, but certainly more often than photographs of Palestinian women from the popular classes. This reflects Jawhariyyeh's overall nationalist, class project.

Our acknowledgement of the relative absence of Arab women should not deflect from the discursive and ideological *manner* by which Palestinian women are made visible or invisible in these albums. At the base, material level, we understand the importance of representation in gender equity and parity. Yet, we also understand that visibility and representation, or the lack therein, fully reflects the distribution of power across and within Palestinian and Arab society and how gendered power systems (i.e. heteropatriarchy) structure them.

For a study that takes photography as its locus of representing not only social history but social relations that bind the colonized societies, this chapter, even if minimally, gestures toward the ways in which the lack of visibility and presence of women in the visual archive serves to distract us from considering the full range of ways the material, social, political, and economic lives of women structure Palestinian and Arab polities. As social products of the urban middle class, no one may be surprised to learn that Jawharriyeh's albums very explicitly reproduce the patriarchy, gender hierarchy, and gender systems in Palestinian Arab society that cut across class and sect. As three male, Arab scholars, we resist complicity with the erasure of women (especially working class women) from this and other visual narratives of Palestine that shore up the assumption that, in a sexist, traditional society, women are separate from political society or local economies or the liberation struggle. Such truisms have been articulated as easily by liberal academics as they have been by Orientalists. Rather, we want to stress that the relative absence of women, and the almost total absence of working class and peasant women (including sex workers and consorts, who figure prominently in Jawharriyeh's memoirs) reproduces the erasure of women as central to social production, as Silvia Federici has taught us. Elsewhere we learn that women were fundamental to the production of indigenous Arab photography but largely left out of the commercial and historical record.[1] Likewise, just as "behind every male photographer is a woman," we must understand Jawhariyyeh's albums as saturated with the presence of women as "behind every factory, behind every school, behind every office or mine there is the hidden work of millions of women who have consumed their life, their labor, producing the labor power that works in those factories, schools, offices, or mines"—or photo albums.[2] Furthermore, while we only broach the topic, we, in our discussions, are beginning to ponder how Jawhariyyeh's visual narrative deflects also from critical and operative practices of women in the *production of Palestinian* history and the resistance to settler colonialism within strategies that navigate, reproduce and/or challenge internal patriarchal frameworks within Palestinian communities.

In addition, thinking about the affective quality of photography in relation to dominant and counter-material histories in conversation and tension with lived contemporary realities may present methods and techniques to exit from the hegemony of the visibility/invisibility binary.[3] Affective theory allows us to draw out the presence of women, labor, and the racialized that saturate images while also being overwritten by dominant representation. We invite scholars and readers, in the future, to consider more rigorously the gender interplay within the narrative, if not the gendered, class, and national overdetermination, that Jawhariyyeh "imagines" and lays out before us, and how that narrative connects with living Palestine today.

The captions provided for these photographs come from a variety of sources, each of which provided different information. We cobble together captions from a number of origins to give coherence, with brevity, to the images that Jawhariyyeh is presenting to us. They are a composite: (a) The original caption that Jawhariyyeh wrote in his albums under each image, provided here in *italics*. (b) After Jawhariyyeh's original information (in italics), we then provide additional information to elaborate on each image, including names of photographers when available to us. (c) We also supply selected further information found in Jawhariyyeh's "index," that is, his notebooks that accompany the albums. Entries into these notebooks are erratic and uneven. His comments for any given image can range from no or a few words up to paragraphs. Therefore, we are discerning about providing information from the index.

FIGURE 3.1. *The demonstration of the Arab ladies [upper class women from the Arab Women's Executive Committee] protesting the announcement by his excellency the High Commissioner following the 1929 Revolt. The house of ʿAwni ʿAbd al-Hadi.* Jawhariyyeh writes that "the demonstration started from the home of lawyer ʿAwni Bey Abd al-Hadi in protest of the statements made by the High Commissioner of Palestine following his return from London, in which he condemned Arab activities, describing them as brutal . . . which in turn led to the strengthening of the Arab revolt. The demonstration was organized by veiled Arab Muslim women along with their Christian sisters. The commissioner retracted and apologized." The wife of ʿAwni, whose name was Tarab (1910–76), appears with Wasif's numbering on the photo as number 1. She was an early female activist in Palestine and one of the founders of the Palestine's Arab Women's Congress. No. 2 is Matiel Mughannam; no. 5 is Nabihah Nasir from Birzeit. Photographer unknown. Jawhariyyeh Album 2, IPS Beirut.

FIGURE 3.2. *Bab al-Khalil from outside [of the Old City] towards the Jerusalem Citadel. You can see al-Ma'arif Café, which was the only theater in Jerusalem, 1900.* The photograph is from the American Colony photo department, and the date Wasif provided might not be exact, since it appears in some archives as from the year 1910. Jawhariyyeh Album 5, IPS Beirut.

FIGURE 3.3. *The meeting held at Rawdat al-Maʾarif in 1930 to debate sending a delegation to England following the revolt of 1929.* Rawdat al-Maʾarif was a school located near the Dome of the Rock. The delegation eventually traveled to London to present its case, calling for an end to British policy regarding Zionist colonization of Palestine. Wasif wrote the names of those appearing in the photograph. Photographer unknown. Jawhariyyeh Album 2, IPS Beirut.

FIGURE 3.4. *A beautiful view of the Dead Sea around the start of the year 1914, during the times of the late Hussein Effendi Al-Husseini and the late Jalal al-din al-'Alami.* Photo: American Colony Photo Department. Jawhariyyeh Album 1, IPS Beirut.

FIGURE 3.5. *Photograph of General Dill, 1937.* General John Dill was sent to Palestine to stop the Arab Revolt of 1936; he was appointed commander of the British forces in Palestine in 1936–37. The High Commissioner, Sir Arthur Wauchope, is to his right, leaving the memorial altar on Jerusalem's Mount Scopus, preceded by the Anglican Bishop, Francis Graham Brown. Photo: American Colony Photo Department. The photo is very likely from 1936, not 1937 as Jawhariyyeh writes. Jawhariyyeh Album 3, IPS Beirut.

FIGURE 3.6. *A historic photograph on the occasion of a political event during the Ottoman period, most likely from the period of the mutasarrif Subhi Bey, appointed on the 10th of September 1324. This date is according to the Ottoman calendar; 1324 is 1907 CE. Subhi Bey is the bearded man third from the right. Photographer unknown. Jawhariyyeh Album 2, IPS Beirut.*

FIGURE 3.7. *His Beatitude the Greek Orthodox Patriarch of Jerusalem in 1899. He was ordained as a patriarch in 1897.* Damianos I (Damian in English) was the patriarch of Jerusalem until his death in 1931. The photo is signed by C. Khouri, though no specific information is known about such a photographer. Jawhariyyeh Album 1, IPS Beirut.

FIGURE 3.8. *Friday flea market [cattle market] next to the pool of al-Sultan in the valley towards the colony of Montefiore and Bab al-Khalil.* In his memoirs, Wasif writes that he was appointed as a municipal animal inspector at the market. Photo: American Colony Photo Department. Jawhariyyeh Album 2, IPS Beirut.

FIGURES 3.9. *Yusuf Dia' al-Din al-Khalidi Pasha. Al-Khalidi (1842—1906) served as a mayor of Jerusalem and as a deputy in the Ottoman Parliament (Majlis al-Mab'uthan).* The photographer is Garabed Krikorian.

FIGURE 3.10. Portrait of a younger Yusuf Dia' al-Din al-Khalidi Pasha by the official photographer of the Armenian Convent, Jerusalem. Jawhariyyeh Album 1, IPS Beirut.

FIGURE 3.11. *The first years at al-Madrasa al-Wataniya al-Dusturiyah (the National Constitutional School in 1908).* The school was a project of educator Khalil Sakakini, who appears seated to the left. Jawhariyyeh Album 2, IPS Beirut.

FIGURE 3.12. *A photograph of the freedom arch at Bab al-Qal'a (the Gate of the Citadel), Jerusalem.* The arch was in celebration of the Ottoman Constitutional Revolution of 1908. Photographer unknown. Jawhariyyeh Album 1, IPS Beirut.

FIGURE 3.13. *Inauguration Ceremony of King George Street in Jerusalem, December 19, 1924. High Commissioner of Palestine Sir Herbert Samuel giving a speech and in attendance Sir Ronald Storrs, the former Governor of Jerusalem, Mayor Raghib Bey al-Nashashibi.* Wasif pointed out in the notebook that behind Samuel stands Wadia al-Shaftari, the first translator in the Mandate Government. Above this is a group portrait of the Postal and Telegraph Department of Jerusalem, 1926. On the lower left we see two anonymous British officers walking with the Jerusalem YMCA in the distance. Jawhariyyeh Album 3, IPS Beirut.

FIGURE 3.14. *'Ali Akram Bey*. 'Ali Akram was the *mutasarrif* (the governor) of the Jerusalem district between 1905 and 1908. Photographer: Garabed Krikorian. Jawhariyyeh Album 1, IPS Beirut.

FIGURE 3.15. *Hakham Bashi* [the chief Rabbi of Jerusalem]. Eliyahu Moshe Panigel (1850–1919) was the Sephardic Rabbi of Jerusalem around 1906. Photographer unknown. Jawhariyyeh Album 1, IPS Beirut Collection.

FIGURE 3.16. *Ramallah Conference in 1908.* The conference, according to the notebook, was held at the Friends School and was in celebration of Ottoman revolt that year. Photographer unknown. Jawhariyyeh Album 1, IPS Beirut Collection.

FIGURE 3.17. *A celebration of the Epiphany on Jordan River in 1905.* More details were provided in the notebook, where the photo is described as "a historic picture of some members of the Arab Orthodox community." Wasif provided the names of all those in the picture. He appears in the picture as the little child wearing a tarboush (fez). Photographer unknown. Jawhariyyeh Album 1, IPS Beirut Collection.

FIGURE 3.18. *Christmas festivities with the entry of his beatitude the Latin Patriarch to the Church of the Nativity in Bethlehem to hold mass.* Photo: The American Colony. Jawhariyyeh Album 5, IPS Beirut Collection.

FIGURE 3.19. *In the aftermath of the 1929 Revolt and the appointment of the Shaw Commission [the official name was the Commission on the Palestine Disturbances of August 1929]. The photograph is in front of al-Buraq [the Wailing/Western Wall], which [the Palestinian delegation was] investigating. In it we see lawyer Subhi al-Khadra, the two British lawyers, one with his wife, Hajj Amin al-Husseini, Ajaj Nuwayhid, Sheikh ʿAraf Yunis, and Sheikh Saʾid al-Khatib.* Photographer unknown. Jawhariyyeh Album 2, IPS Beirut.

FIGURE 3.20. *Bedouin woman in traditional dress.* In the American Colony records at the Library of Congress. The subject is described as "a woman from the settled town of Kerak, Jordan, who probably was the wife of a sheikh. Her high social status is reflected in her expensive clothing (which possibly came from Homs, Syria) and her hair braids. Braids were predominantly worn by Christian women of the tribes of Jordan." Jawhariyyeh Album 6. IPS Beirut.

FIGURE 3.21. *As it was: the hill of Bab al-Khalil in the year 1909.* Photographer unknown. Jawhariyyeh Album 1, IPS Beirut.

FIGURE 3.22. A page from Album 1 that shows members of Arab Orthodox community who were designated to carry the flag of their clan (*sanjak*) during the celebration of Holy Fire at the Church of the Holy Sepulcher on the Saturday before Easter. They are Saliba Abu Zakhariya (upper left), unknown portrait (lower left), Spiro al-Qarah (middle), and Niqula Ansarah (lower right). Jawhariyyeh Album 1, IPS Beirut.

FIGURE 3.23. *British army train from Jerusalem heading north, near the Tombs of the Kings, 1918.* The military train line that existed at the end of World War I linked Jerusalem to the region north of Ramallah, and the lines were extended to al-Balu' area, in al-Bireh (al-Birah) and beyond, bringing soldiers and military hardware to the retreating Ottoman front in the spring of 1918. The British dismantled the train after the war, in 1919. Photo: American Colony Photo Department. Jawhariyyeh Album 1, IPS Beirut.

FIGURE 3.24. *The Muslim Palestinian National Party in 1932.* In that year two Islamic conferences were held in Jerusalem. The first was known as "The Islamic General Conference" and was hosted by the Mufti, Hajj Amin al-Husseini. The second, shown here, was a response from the opposition to the Mufti and was known as the conference of the Palestinian Muslim Nation, led by Raghib Nashashibi, shown in the middle. Photographer unknown. Jawhariyyeh Album 2, IPS Beirut.

FIGURE 3.25. *Another view seen from the revolution of 1929 in front of the post office.* In the notebooks Wasif added: "The beginning of the revolution of 1929 in front of the post office on Jaffa road, after the funeral of a Jew, August 15, 1929." The revolution is what is more commonly known in Arabic as al-Buraq revolution and in English as the Walling Wall riots. The image shows Zionist settlers from Ze'ev Jabotinsky right-wing Revisionist Alliance, congregating after the funeral of a Zionist settler. Photographer unknown. Jawhariyyeh Album 3, IPS Beirut.

FIGURE 3.26. *His majesty King George VI (with the Duke of Kent [his younger brother]) with Abdallah [Emir of Transjordan].* Photographer unknown. Jawhariyyeh Album 3, IPS Beirut.

FIGURE 3.27. *A court in Jerusalem. In attendance: Ahmad al-Ja'uni, Jirji Zakariyah, Faidi al-'Alami, Musa Bayk 'Aqel, Matia Saraphim.* This was the Bidaya court (first instance or lower court) in Jerusalem. Photographer unknown. Jawhariyyeh Album 2, IPS Beirut.

FIGURE 3.28. *An Indian guard searching passersby for weapons at Bab al-Khalil after the revolt of 1920.* Photographer unknown, though very likely Khalil Raad. Jawhariyyeh Album 2, IPS Beirut.

FIGURE 3.29. *The first Arab delegation to London in 1921 protesting the ominous Balfour Declaration. Ibrahim Shammas [seated from the right], Musa Kazhim Pasha al-Husseini [in the middle], Hajj Adel Hammad [seated on the left], Amin al-Tamimi [standing on the right], Shibli al-Jamal [standing in the middle], and Mu'in (Mouin) al-M'adi.* Photographer unknown. Jawhariyyeh Album 2, IPS Beirut.

FIGURE 3.30. *Opening ceremony of the first durable bridge over the Jordan River, 1310 AH [1893 CE].* Photographer unknown. Jawhariyyeh Album 1, IPS Beirut.

FIGURE 3.31. *At the plaza of al-Haram [the Sanctuary] in 1931.* Although Wasif numbered the individuals in the photograph, he did not list their names. Photographer unknown. Jawhari-yyeh Album 2, IPS Beirut.

FIGURE 3.32. *His Majesty King Faisal I and Tahsin Qadri in 1932.* It is unknown if the photograph was taken in Jerusalem. King Faisal was the Hashemite king of Iraq. Tahsin Qadri was a prominent figure in Arab politics at the time and the king's military attaché. The king's last visit to Jerusalem was in 1933. It is possible that the date provided by Wasif is incorrect. Jawhariyyeh Album 1, IPS Beirut.

4

Patronage and Photography

Hussein Hashim's Melancholic Journey

Salim Tamari

The story of Wasif's life in Jerusalem and his relationship with the Husseini family is a record of Jerusalem's patrician families and their cultural milieu (fig. 4.1). His adventures, recorded in his memoirs and more vividly in his photographic albums, are also a celebration of spectacles—the changing urban landscape, the city's ceremonial activities, the musical and theatrical scene, and the greatest spectacle of all—the events leading to military collapse and the fall of the city into British hands. Wasif Jawhariyyeh, unlike his father, was at once an observer of these events—as a man of leisure, a *flâneur*—as well as a reluctant participant.

Jawhariyyeh was educated in Orthodox, missionary, and state institutions, allowing him to traverse the class boundaries between the city's elite communities and its plebeians, as well as the communitarian boundaries between its Muslims, Christians, and Jews. The background to Wasif's musical training was his involvement in the city's religious ceremonials, and the increasingly secularized public space of seasonal celebrations. He became intimately involved with visiting musical performers from Egypt, Salameh Hijazi and Badi'a Masabni in particular. He also developed his performative talents through involvement with the earliest theatrical spectacles: the magic box, the shadow theatre (*karakoz/karakuz*), and the cinematograph. As an amateur musician Jawhariyyeh commuted between a number of different groups in Palestine, interacting with locals but also Arab and foreign musicians who passed through the "Holy Land." Over a period of four decades (1910–48) he kept photographic mementos from these events which evolved into his albums (fig. 4.2).

The discussion of Jawhariyyeh's photographic albums in this section is inspired by Susan Sontag's seminal essay "Melancholy Objects," published as part of *On*

FIGURE 4.1. Mayor Hussein Hashim in his prime, Jerusalem, 1907. Photographer: Khalil Raad. Jawhariyyeh Album 1, IPS Beirut.

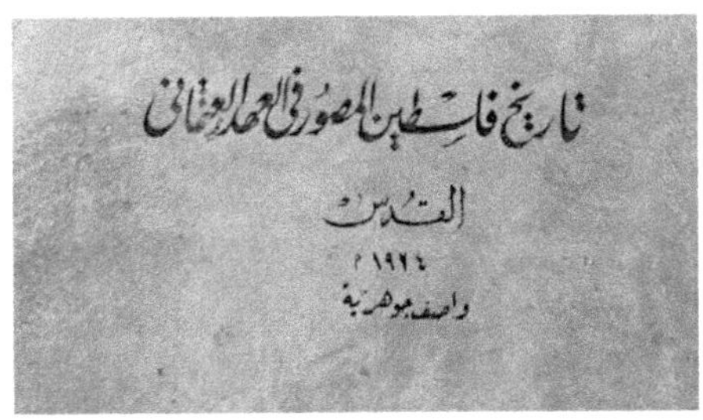

FIGURE 4.2. Cover of Volume 1 of Wasif Jawhariyyeh's photographic albums. Athens Collection.

Photography. In this collection of essays on the relevance of photographic images to our time, Sontag notes that photography is surreal at its core, and that specifically what is surreal "is the distance imposed, and bridged, by the photograph: the social distance and the distance in time."[1] According to Sontag,

> photography inevitably entails a certain patronizing of reality. From being 'out there,' the word comes to be 'inside' photographs . . . [the] contingency of photographs confirms that everything is perishable; the arbitrariness of photographic evidence indicates that reality is fundamentally unclassifiable. Reality is summed up in an array of casual fragments—an endlessly alluring, poignantly reductive way of dealing with the world.[2]

"The origin" of the melancholic condition is "that which is born of distance"—that is, "a separation from reality"—while such a "distance may be temporal, spatial, political or cultural."[3] In Jawhariyyeh's world this distancing comes from the rupture created between the images he collected of Jerusalem and its people before and during the Great War (and later the 1948 expulsion) and the seeming tranquility of the urban scene that emerged during the colonial period. For him, as evidenced from his memoirs, "the real" Palestine is what existed before the war and before the *Nakba*.

Wasif Jawhariyyeh is best understood not as a collector of photographic images, ouds, and musical paraphernalia, but as a flaneur gazing on his changing world of spectacles. In this regard, he was a product of Arab modernity, replete with social contradictions, political rivalries, and class tensions and allegiances that prominently appear where comparing the differences between the visual narrative of his photography albums and the written narrative of his memoirs. Three such "spectacles" will be discussed here. The first is the ceremonial spectacle: Wasif's ethnographic depictions of Nabi Musa, the outings of the Virgin Mary in Sheikh Jarrah, and the greatest ceremonial event of the city, the "Saturday of light" as the throngs converge on the Holy Sepulcher in the Old City to witness and partake of the light of resurrection. The second is the performative spectacle of the magic box, *Karakoz* (shadow theater), and the cinematograph. And finally we see the surrender of Jerusalem as a war spectacle, loaded with ceremony, eyewitnesses, and public panic anticipating collapse.

As a chronicler and collector, Jawhariyyeh attempted in his albums to create an order out these disparate images through temporal and thematic cataloguing. Although the bulk of his photographic collection is preoccupied with an inventory of the city's leading notables and grandees, as well as the ceremonial events that marked the tempo of religious and seasonal celebrations of the city (Nabi Musa, Sitna Mariam, Nabi Ayyub, Ramadan, Simon the Just), there is also a considerable focus on the quotidian that distinguishes him from other observers of the city at the turn of the century. Several features of this quotidian interest appear in the collection. One is the minute detail given to popular professions: builders, lawyers, entertainers, stonemasons, policemen, and so on. Another are the spectacles of street life—theatrical musicians, performers, dancers, dramatic performances, and the cinematograph. As the city became an arena of military operations during World War I, the albums devote considerable space to the military, not only with portraits of officers and generals, but also battle scenes, workers digging trenches, enemy (British) prisoners, and the hanging of deserters. The album also displays the iconic images of the surrender of Jerusalem by commander Zaki Bey and Mayor Husseini—Wasif's patron and friend—together with a detailed listing of the local people involved that appears nowhere in the historical record except in Jawhariyyeh's album.

Both Jawhariyyeh's memoirs and his photographic collection challenge the long-held notion that Jerusalem was divided into ethnic and religious quarters (Armenian, Jewish, Christian, and Muslim *harat*). His social relations with the Husseini family, coupled with his cultural enterprises as a musician, meant that he can portray a city with a distinct Jerusalemite communal identity that grew and competed with other identities at the time. It is the visual narrative of Jawhariyyeh's photographs that give dimension to this dynamic, changing social life that abruptly ended in 1948.

Women are strikingly absent from much of Wasif's photographic narrative. In a sequence of photographs of the national movement he did catalogue five images of a "women's demonstration" from 1929 following the Buraq incidents. Five of the women are identified.[4] Although his world is full of female entertainers, such as the singer and dancer Badi'a Masabni—and his narrative about his family life, and the domestic life of the city's aristocracy and middle classes, is also populated by women—they rarely appear in the photographic collection. His diary is replete with references to mistresses and concubines of the Husseinis, the Khalidis, the Nashashibis, and other members of the city's elite, and to female singers, oud players, and sex workers, yet nowhere do we have an image of those women. The only exception is Um Kalthum, during her occasional tours of the city, and Masabni, by whose performance he was mesmerized. It is as if he was protecting his own sisters and daughters from exposure, as well as the reader from being scandalized by his narrative. Only in the private section of the Athens collection do we gain access to some of these women.

One of the major challenges in unraveling Wasif's visual discourse is to establish the correspondence between the Jawhariyyeh diary/memoir and the photographic albums. This correspondence can be easily established when Wasif is discussing the profiles of his colleagues and contemporary acquaintances and political figures. The albums are profusely annotated for these personalities. The author was keen at providing captions, as well as detailed commentaries on places and events. This is true for major political and military figures in the Ottoman period, as well as for musical colleagues and entertainers who visited or worked with Wasif, such as Sheikh 'Umar al-Batsh, Muhammad Abd al-Wahab, and Badi'a Masabni. Similarly, the albums are replete in documenting his relationship with the Husseinis—Haj Salim and his son Hussein in particular. A number of images identify the houses and farms of Khirbat 'Amr, in which Wasif's father was the Husseinis' bailiff. The Husseini mansions in Jerusalem (in the Old City, in Sheikh Jarrah, and in Bab al-Sahirah) are also documented. But again, we do not have a portrait of the mistress/concubine Persephone, despite the substantive material on her history—nor on any of the wives, daughters, or female companions of the Jerusalem aristocracy.

Military events, army processions, battle scenes, and the hanging of 'traitors' are also well documented. Some of these photographs are rare and unique, such as the exceptional meeting of the Red Crescent Society during the war in 1915, presided over by Hussein Hashim, and attended by leading Jewish, Muslim, and Christian Jerusalemites. The albums provide us with a very rich repertoire of ceremonial events, including Nabi Musa and Sitna Mariam celebrations. The

FIGURE 4.3. In this photograph from the Athens Collection, dated 1915, Jawhariyyeh marks his presence (number 11 in red) in the crowd watching the execution of a deserter. This indication of his presence at the hanging differs from the IPS Collection in Beirut. (See Figure. 2.7). Athens Collection.

albums, however, suffer from some major omissions in illustrating artistic and performative events in Jerusalem during both the Ottoman and Mandate periods. This is particularly irritating given the frequent references to and discussion of these events, which include traditional theater (*karagoz*, musical operettas), concerts, and street bands. To compensate, we have resorted to using contemporary alternate photographs, as well as the occasional sketch. (For example, I have used World War I-era photographs of local bordellos from the Albert Kahn collection, and Ottoman Turkish sketches for the karagoz performances.)

I Am Neither a Writer Nor a Historian

Wasif Jawhariyyeh commences his three-volume Jerusalem memoirs with his usual sense of false modesty—"I am neither a respected littérateur, nor a historian, nor a travel writer . . . but only a simple civil servant who was barely able to finish his initial schooling during the Great War."[5] He then goes on to demonstrate why he possesses all of those skills, in addition to his primary reputation as a virtuoso musician and oud player. While he is discussing the circumstances of his birth, and his naming after Judge Wasif Bey al-'Azim, we are introduced to the beginning of his photographic collection. "My birthday was on a Wednesday morning at the beginning of January 1897 by the Julian calendar (14th Gregorian), which is the New Year for the Eastern Christians. . . . My father named me after his friend

FIGURE 4.4. Meeting of the Red Crescent Society, Jerusalem 1915. Another picture of Wasif Jawhariyyeh surreptitiously inserting himself in a public event. He is seen here in the upper right corner, marked as no. 7. Mayor Husseini is no. 5 in the center. Album 1, p. 51, Athens Collection.

Wasif Bey al-'Azim, who was at the time the head of the Jerusalem Cassation Court (*Isti'naf*). I still have his beautiful portrait which he presented to my father, which I later preserved in the Jawhariyyeh Collection."[6]

The seven albums—annotated, captioned, and indexed during the 1950s—are organized thematically and chronologically by the author of the memoirs. They contain portraits of governors, military commanders, judges, lawyers, mayors, musicians, entertainers, police officers, and many others from his lifetime. Many of these images were dedicated to Jawhariyyeh by their subjects. They also include cityscapes, buildings, street scenes, and public events. During the war Wasif added military parades, public hangings, and war casualties from the front (fig. 4.3). He rarely included images of himself or his family; one picture does include Wasif attending a function of the Red Crescent Society when the city's patricians were organizing a fundraising event for the Ottoman war effort (fig. 4.4). In addition to his photographic albums, the collection includes a large number of musical instruments (mostly *ouds*), mother of pearl artwork, local crafts, and religious paraphernalia. The latter included icons painted by Wasif's father for the Rum Orthodox Church.[7]

THE *FLÂNEUR* OF JERUSALEM AND HIS SPECTACLES: A VISUAL CULTURE OF THE EARLY 1900S

The relationship of photography to the notion of spectacle and the spectacular has been influenced by Guy Debord's *Society of the Spectacle*—which describes how capitalist modernity has degraded social life by replacing all experienced phenomena into its representation, meaning that experience loses its vitality by being reified.[8] The principle of commodity fetishism becomes the framing principle; in this that "the domination of society by 'intangible as well as tangible things' reaches its absolute fulfillment in the spectacle, where the tangible world is replaced by a selection of images which exist above it, and which simultaneously impose themselves as the tangible par excellence."[9] In an essay on "photographic spectacle," Phil Carney modifies Debord's idea suggesting that the incorporation of "the social practice of performance" allows the audience to be an "active receiver of spectacle" and simultaneously "engage in social practices that feed back into . . . forces of performance."

> [T]he photographic spectacle . . . is a multiplicity that produces flows of forces working in the registers of the cultural, the social, the inter-individual and the unconscious. When the word spectacle is used here, it also embraces those important festive dynamics in which the audience is both an active receiver of spectacle and, at the same time, engages in social practices that feed back into its forces of performance. That said, we cannot reduce these social practices to individual performance, even if this also undoubtedly plays its role. Nor, from a political viewpoint, should we use this model as an excuse for imagining that festivity is a micropolitical phenomenon reducible to individual, conscious, liberal agency.[10]

Indeed, Debord's observations about the society of the spectacle may be anachronistic in thinking about visual culture, the entrenchment of capitalism, and social reproduction in Mandate Palestine. However, Carney's expansion of the theory of the spectacle seems relevant, especially in his introduction of the voyeuristic element through the character of the flaneur. Here he identifies the flaneur with the modern spectator (after Benjamin), which, in our case, recalls the voyeuristic features in Wasif's relationship to his albums. As Carney describes, "the modern spectator is a physically active, mobile figure who is part of the urban spectacle. Amid this spectacle, and contributing to its forms and forces, there arises the circulating photograph, ushering in a new image world. The urban crowd mixed in architectural space but also in the new spaces opened up by the photographic world."[11]

But Wasif, as flaneur, is both a voyeur and performer. He is (was) mesmerized by watching travelling players, and he often saw himself jumping into the performance—both as a singer and instrumentalist—although we have little to inform us how the audience reacted to these intrusions. Jawhariyyeh was an avid follower of the theatrical scene in Palestine. He participated as both viewer and performer in his own musical *takht* (band), where he played the *'oud*. A significant portion of his memoirs narrates the details of visiting musical performances, in particular travelling theatrical groups from Egypt. His album includes an image of a stage adorned with an Ottoman imperial flag outside Jerusalem's Notre Dame building, where a play was performed to benefit the Ottoman Red Crescent in 1917. The same image, with similar captions, appears in the Matson Collection now housed at the Library of Congress, indicating that this is an American Colony photograph.

Other major sources were the famous Jerusalemite portrait photographer M. Savides, and Khalil Raad's studio photographs. From the latter Jawhariyyeh acquired many images of Ottoman war propaganda which Raad had been commissioned to produce.[12]

Wasif's memoirs, *al-Quds al-'Uthmaniyah*, are a virtual ethnographic tour of Jerusalem, buttressed by photographic images that attempt to capture his narrative. The focus is the modernity of the Old City at the end of the Ottoman period, and a record of his adventures during the Mandate.[13] The seven-volume unpublished photographic albums, which he titled *Tarikh Falastin al-Mussawar fil-'Ahd al-'Uthmani*, and their annotated index, were meant as a visual accompaniment to his memoirs. Jawhariyyeh consciously organized his writings so that the memoirs correspond to the photographic albums. The index lists the serialized images in the albums, indicating the theme and a short description of the image, either by name or event. He placed a question mark or an indication of uncertainty next to the images of forgotten faces. Parallel to the index, Wasif created an annotated log of each photograph with extensive details about the person or event, along with a listing of names, dates, and circumstances that accompanied the photograph. Jawhariyyeh annotated the images in white ink on a black background; these extensive annotations are invaluable not only for illustrating the memoirs, but also as an explanatory note for the circumstances in which the photographs were taken, although only a few include the name of the photographer. These annotations, however are not systematic, and for a large number of these events described we need to rely on secondary sources to explain their background. An example of this rich record can be gleaned from the author's comment on a photo of the launching of a speedboat meant for the Dead Sea at the Notre Dame headquarters of the Jerusalem garrison (called Manzil in Turkish), which included filming it as propaganda for the Ottoman war effort (fig. 4.5).[14] This image of the speedboat was part of a larger repertoire of military parades that appear in the second album, corresponding to Wasif's own involvement with the army as a "naval officer" in the Dead Sea during the same period.

Jawhariyyeh's sensuous tour of Jerusalem begins with a street mapping of the sounds and smells of the Old City food and spice shops, and the various chants and melodies of food sellers. During the great famine of 1915/1916, he wrote his famous ode to hunger, appropriately titled "*karshat*" (tripe fillings), which evokes all the absent local dishes in melodic rhyme. He sardonically describes the ditty as having become "the national anthem of Palestine" (fig. 4.6). *Karshat* was one of two compositions written by Wasif that has survived, and the only one whose music score is available.[15] Although it is not included in his *Musical Notebook*, we are lucky to have a live recording of the piece that was preserved from the archives of Beirut Radio in the 1950s.[16] In this piece we gain a singular access to Wasif's rich baritone voice and playful oud.

FIGURE 4.5. *A picture of the first naval launch brought by the Ottoman army from Jaffa to the Notre Dame building, which was converted by the Turks into the Manzil Mufattishlji Headquarters for the Ottoman Army, under the leadership of Qa'im Maqam Brinci 'Ali Rushan Bey, who is seen here on top of the boat next to his assistant Nihad Bey along with other staff members of the Manzil. This launch was sent to aid [Mayor] Hussein Hashim al-Husseini, who was contracted to build a harbor on the [Eastern shores] of the Dead Sea during the tenure of the late Muhyi al-Din al-Husseini and Sheikh Jalal al-Din al-'Alami. The harbor was commissioned by Rushan Bey in order to transport grain from Transjordan via the Dead Sea under the administration of Mayor Husseini (details in my memoirs, p. 237). Through my association with Hussein Effendi I had spent considerable time with Rushan Bey. I have recorded several of these anecdotes in 226, 241 and 262 in my manuscript.* Jawhariyyeh Album 1, IPS Beirut. Notes from Jawhariyyeh's Album Index, 137.

FIGURE 4.6. "Karshat—".Wasif Jawhariyyeh's ode to the famine of 1915, which, he claimed, became the "National Anthem of Palestine." Source: Yusra Jawhariyah 'Arnitah, *al-Funun al-sha' biyah fi Filastin* (1998).

FIGURE 4.7. Inauguration of Jamal Pasha Blvd. Jaffa, 1916. Athens Collection.

CEREMONIALS AND THE CONQUEST
OF PUBLIC SPACE

The photographic albums cover two sets of public ceremonials. The first introduce the viewer to the inauguration of public buildings, gardens, boulevards, and military processions—especially during wartime. Two significant images introduce us to public responses to the Ottoman constitutional revolution of 1908, celebrated as the festival of *Hurriyat* (freedom). The first is a unique picture of Governor 'Ali Akram Bey addressing a huge throng of demonstrators in Jaffa's Clock Square—arguably the first image of a mass public demonstration in Palestine. The second is a portrait of Jerusalem's notables and public officials holding Ottoman flags and CUP banners, with the slogans of "Freedom, Equality and Justice"—also from 1908. The second image is clearly a publicly organized event and lacks the spontaneity and the popular character of the Jaffa demonstration.

The second set of ceremonial images are centered around religious processionals and saints' holidays (known as *mawasim*) (fig. 4.7). Those images are discussed in elaborate details in the two-volume memoirs, which contain detailed ethnographic engagement with the *mawasim* and their communal hymns and celebratory dances—Nabi Musa, Bir Ayyub, Sitna Mariam, Purim—culminating in the greatest communal celebration of the holy city—*Sabt al-Nur* (the Saturday of Fire), which in the Eastern Orthodox tradition ushers in the resurrection of Jesus.

FIGURE 4.8. Theatrical performance in aid of the Ottoman Red Crescent, 1917 (Notre Dame building, Jerusalem). This was one of several images used by Jawhariyyeh from the American Colony Collection. Jawhariyyeh Album 1, IPS Beirut.

Wasif's ceremonial ethnography is particularly valuable in demonstrating the emergence of a secularized public space from the convergence of communal religious celebrations. This can be seen in his description of "Shat'hat Sittna Maryam" (The Virgin Mary's Outing) in Sheikh Jarrah and the Mount of Olives—and the Bir Ayyub Outing (*shat-ha*) in the Silwan spring in early April. Here Jerusalemites enjoyed the odors of the blossoming of jasmine, and of lemon trees, "mixed with the aromas of the open sewers of the holy city".[17]

HAKAWATI AND SHADOW PLAY (*KARAGOZ*)

For all his preoccupation with the performative theatre, and his substantial writings about it, the Jawhariyyeh albums have few images on these performances. There are two or three photographs of the Manshiyah Café, and al-Ma'arif Café at Bab al-Khalil where, he claims the first shadow theatre was performed. We also have an image of "an Ottoman theater" from the Manzil at the Notre Dame building, where benefit shows for the Red Crescent were viewed (fig. 4.8). Wasif also collected a number of publicity images used by the Fourth Army for their cinematographic propaganda (fig. 4.5). We have a number of portraits of singers, dancers and musicians such as Badi'a Masabni and Sheikh 'Umar al-Batsh, his oud teacher—but not much else in terms of visuals for these performances.

Wasif was particularly fond of the operettas of Salameh Hijazi (such as *Antony and Cleopatra*) and cabaret sketches by Egyptian stars such as Masabni and Najib Rihani. The performances included local school renditions of classical Arabic love ballads (e.g. *'Antar wa 'Abla*), as well as patriotic theatrical performances based on major battles from Islamic history (the conquest of Andalusia, or Salah al-Din's liberation of Jerusalem). The local censor intervened and banned performances which were seen as fermenting Arab separatist sentiments.[18] Besides the local theater, Wasif highlights three visual performances that dominated the visual culture at the turn of the century: *Sunduq al-'Ajab* (the Magic Box); *karakoz* (shadow puppets), and the Cinematograph.

A popular form of traditional art in Jerusalem was *al-hakawati* (the storyteller). Those were normally winter performances in the larger cafés of the Old City. The *hakawati* would be an informally trained storyteller with a repertoire of classical Arabic literature, usually recited in colloquial or mixed Arabic. He would sit on an elevated platform in the café and recite (or read) to the seated audience on straw chairs. The most popular performances, in Wasif's Jerusalem, were recitations of *Amir Amara*, *'Antar wa 'Abla*, and the ballads of *Abu Zayd al-Hilali*, all of them related to chivalry in early Islamic periods.[19] Jawhariyyeh can be seen as a literary *hakawati* of Jerusalem's modernity, narrating the story of earlier *hakawatis*.

> Haj Jawdat bin Musa al-Halabi was one of the better-known performers in Jerusalem. He used to perform in Café Abd al-Latif in Bab Hutta. He was very popular and people would attend his performances from as far as Upper Baq'a, weathering the cold and the rain. He used to impersonate the heroes of his tales, completely identifying with them. He used to perform episodes from *Antara* and from *Amir Amara* in installments, to keep his audiences coming every night until the story was finished by the end of the month. The themes of his stories were honor, dignity, resistance to oppression, and revenge against aggressors.[20]

The main competition to the *hakawatis* were the shadow play performances, known in Arabic as *khayal al-dhil*, or *karakoz*, a local slanting of the Persian-Turkish *Karagoz* (fig. 4.9). Those were mainly Ramadan events, although there is evidence that they were performed in other seasons. *Karakoz* performances invariably involve a contestation of wit between the educated Uwaz and his simpleton companion Karakoz. Throughout the Ottoman Sultanate Uwaz (aka Hacivat) represented the literati, while Karakoz was the simple peasant, speaking the local dialect. In many of the regional provinces, such as the Greek and Balkan regions, Hacivat became the Ottoman bureaucrat, while Karakoz would take on the character of a local peasant. Within the Arab world Ibn Danyal popularized the genre in Mameluke Cairo in his play *Tayf al-Khayal*.[21] Over the centuries of performance, the characters and the themes of the play went through several transformations, subject often to local contingencies and local dialects. In the late nineteenth century, and possibly before, the plays contained a substantial degree of libidinous class con-

FIGURE 4.9. Ma'arif Café, located outside the Citadel of Jerusalem, 1900. This was the earliest theatre in Jerusalem, where musical and shadow play (karakoz) were performed. Jawhariyyeh Album 1, IPS Beirut.

flict, but with the rise of ethnic tensions in the Empire, local performances (especially in the Balkans) began to contain contestations between national groups.

Shadow theatre was extremely licentious in the presentation of its plots, breaking all taboos on sexuality, pederasty, and bawdy situations, which may explain why only men attended these shows.[22] Although the censor began to interfere and regulate these performances after the introduction of press laws in 1876, and again after the constitutional reforms of 1908, much of their daring flavor remain evident in existing texts from both Anatolia and the Arab provinces.[23] Karagoz performances were still common in Palestine in the early twentieth century. 'Ali Hasan al-Bawab lists a number of these plays at the Nabi Rubin festival south of Jaffa, which continued to attract audiences until the summer of 1946.[24] In the Jerusalem performances Uwaz speaks with an eloquent classical Arabic, with an occasional dose of Turkish, while Karakoz speaks in the peasant dialect. At the end of each episode the popular wit of the peasant, though impulsive, prevails against the level-headed, but pompous, Uwaz.[25]

Jawhariyyeh preserved extended excerpts from several *karakoz* plays from the Great War period: "The Beggars," "The Butcher," "The Drunkard," and the *Fat'h al-Bakht* ("Reading the Future").[26] In his memoirs Jawhariyyeh also provided long excerpts from two popular shadow play performances: "The Frankish Poodle" (a satire on European domestic animals), and "the Samman" (the Ghee seller).[27]

A shadow play involved wooden puppets manipulated by the master storyteller against a screen; the figures would have been illuminated by candle or kerosene lamp. The master pantomime performer was called *karakozati* in Arabic.[28] During Ramadan in Jerusalem five performances took place one hour after the breaking of the fast. The first three 'acts' were for children, while the last two were for adult audiences.[29] Wasif lists the major cafés where these performances took place: Khalil Nijam Café, Bab Hutta Café, Wad Café (opposite the Austrian Hospice), and Khan al-Zeit Café. All early performances were for children. The major play for adults was performed in 'Ali Izhiman Café (also in the Wad neighborhood), and was attended by literary figures such as Sheikh Muhammad al-Salih (director of al-Ma'aref school), Ustaz Nakhlah Zureik (Zurayq), Sheikh 'Ali Rimawi (editor of the Ottoman Gazette, *al-Quds al-Sharif*), Khalil Sakakini (founder of al-Dusturiyah College), and the poet Is'af al-Nashashibi. The most famous shadow player in that period was the Tripolitanian poet Haj Mahmud al-Karakozati and his fellow performers.

> The Karkoz 'tent' in Izhiman's café was a large sheet of white linen behind which Haj Mahmud manipulated the puppets with the assistance of his helper, a man known as Abd al-Salam al-Aqra ('the bold') who played the riqa and launched the play with a muwashhah '*Ya Hilalal Ghab Anni wa-htajab*' (the Crescent Disappeared and Became Invisible). Mahmud then dangles the puppet of Karakoz, whose shadow begins to dance on al-Aqra's music. Haj Mahmud was performing while smoking the *nargilah*, which rarely left his mouth throughout the evening. When the play was finished he would rush to the main exit of the café and start collecting the *matlik* [Ottoman penny] from the exiting audience, while joking with them in different languages. If Ramadan happened to come during the summer, then the main performance would take place in the Nabulsi Café, owned by the Hindiyah family, outside the Damascus gate. Those festivities began just after midnight and would often continue until the cannon fire announced the beginning of fasting in the early morning.[30]

The Magic Lantern (*al-fanus al-sihri)* was introduced into Palestine by studio photographers who were using stereoscope images to cater to tourists and pilgrims. It was a modern version of *karakoz* that was lacking in the latter's imaginative theatricals. The slides were projected on a screen using luxe lamps, and after 1915, electric bulbs. The audience for the magic lantern was a more educated clientele, and the subjects, for local viewers, were mostly landscapes of areas that were inaccessible, and therefore, exotic. In Jerusalem, the magic lantern was introduced by the German Schniller school, and in the American Colony compound, for students and teachers. Wasif tells us in his memoirs that "we were able to see places in the Arab lands we could not travel. In particular we were able to 'visit' Petra, Wadi Musa, Wadi al-Mujib, the Tongue (*lisan*) of the Dead Sea, Ba'albak, and many other places. Ustaz Elias Haddad, the teacher at the Schniller school, would provide us with a running commentary on those scenes."[31] Obviously, this was a pedagogical experience, which was lacking in the imagination and theatrical narratives of the *karakoz* plays. For schools it provided an early form of alternative tourism.

FIGURE 4.10. *Sunduq al-ʿajab*, Jerusalem, c. 1910. This is one of Khalil Raad's most reprinted photographs. Wasif Jawhariyyeh collected Raad's images, often without attribution. Archives, IPS Beirut.

Sunduq al-ʿajab (the Magic Box) was ancestor of the magic lantern, also known as the Persian Box (*sunduq al-ʿajam*). For poorer children, and some adults, this was the cinema of the nineteenth and early twentieth centuries. I myself caught the tail end of the life of this contraption in the early fifties in Ramallah. The box was immortalized by an iconic photograph by Khalil Raad, displayed prominently in the Athens version of the Jawhariyyeh collection (fig. 4.10). The *sunduq* was a semi-circular wooden closet, which (normally) had six external lenses. Inside the box the *hakawati* would control a series of connected drawings on a cylindrical roll, and narrate (or chant) the traditional ballad that appeared on the screen. The viewers (aged five to fifteen) would sit on wooden stools and follow the story. For one *matlik*, or half a piaster, the viewer would receive a fifteen-minute show with some extra vignettes of scenery from around the world.

تع اتفرج وشوف يا سلام شوف احوالك على التمام

This is Egypt. These are the pyramids. This is Abu al-Hul (the Sphinx).
The great wonder. Come habibi take a look.

Sunduq al-ʿajab would move from one neighborhood to another during the holidays, including the *mawasim* of Jerusalem. In order to protect it from the evil eye the *hakawati* would add a head of garlic and blue beads to the flower ornaments.

FIGURE 4.11. Still from the Lumiere brothers, "Leaving the Jerusalem Train Station," 1897.

THE CINEMATOGRAPH

At the turn of the century, the Holy Land was the subject of some of the earliest motion picture projects outside Europe. The cinematograph was the name given to both the camera and the projector of the moving images on the screen. The Lumière brothers, inventors of the cinematograph, made two of the earliest films in history in Palestine: *La Palestina* (1896), and *Leaving the Jerusalem Train Station* (1897) (fig. 4.11).[32] Both contain substantial footage of street life in Jerusalem. Much later, during the war, Albert Kahn sent a team of French photographers to film color images of the Middle East "before it was taken over by modernity."[33] The films included extensive footages of daily life in Istanbul, Beirut, Izmir, and Jerusalem. They also included rare pictures of bordellos in Jerusalem, Jaffa, and Beirut.

Wasif narrates how he attended his first cinematograph event in 1910 when he was a student in Khalil Sakakini's Wataniyah College, in the company of his friends from the Muna family (the current owners of the Educational Bookshop). He recalls,

> The projection was in the theater in the Veikold Building, opposite the Russian Compound on Jaffa Street. The ticket cost one Turkish *bishlik*. The films were all silent, but still it left us with a sense of astonishment. . . . To us children, this perfectly made picture seemed to be of real men, women, and animals, and the small objects represented also seemed real in a way that caused both puzzlement and admiration, for this was like a miniature version of today's cinema.[34]

During the 1920s and 1930s, the number of cinemas in Jerusalem, Jaffa, and Haifa mushroomed. Cinemas became the main locales for both theatrical productions and concerts. Um Kulthum's first performance in Jerusalem was in in 1929 at the Aden Cinema.[35] Leaflets and billboards, reproduced by Wasif in his memoirs, advertised these occasions (fig. 4.12). Abdul Wahhab ('Abd al-Wahhab) performed at Cinema Zion, while Rex Cinema, located near the Mamilla cemetery, was a favored site for other visiting musicians.[36]

FIGURE 4.12. Um Kalthum concert flyer for a performance in Cinema Eden, Jerusalem, October 8, (1926?). Source: Jawhariyyeh, *Storyteller of Jerusalem*, 86.

Wasif narrates how Jewish and Arab audiences were mesmerized by Abdul Wahhab's appearance in person, which was often followed by a cinematic appearance. The following episode (undated, but most likely this took place in the late 1930s) conveys the manner in which Jerusalem audiences interacted with visiting performers.

Abdul Wahab made a second visit to Jerusalem and, being a close friend of the Prince of Poets, Ahmad Shawqi, he stayed at the home of Mr. Is'af al-Nashashibi in Sheikh Jarrah. Muhammad Abdul Wahab was already a glowing star, thanks to the wonderful music, art, and singing that he had given the world and which had moved the souls of both men and women, whether music connoisseurs or not, all over the Arab countries. He thus shot to fame and became indeed one of the greatest music masters we know. He pioneered the introduction of more *tarab* instruments and of Western musical instruments into his orchestra, which added to the beauty and perfection of his music, and people began to savor and appreciate his singing, now that they had become accustomed to his innovative music.

The master decided to give his concert at Cinema Zion on Jaffa Road in Jerusalem. The demand for tickets was so high that there ended up being more people standing than sitting. I was in the front row, waiting impatiently for him to come on stage. The audience received a massive shock with news of the death of the honorable and much-loved judge, the late great 'Ali Bey Jarallah. I thought to myself that, indeed, calamities fall on the calmest nights, while everyone else just froze, for the deceased had been so dear to them. He was an extraordinary person, and his death was a great and irredeemable loss for the people of Jerusalem.[37]

Jawhariyyeh's photographic memory of this concert, and several other similar events, takes precedence in his memoirs over other political events that were taking place at the same time. In this case it is worth quoting at length from Wasif's description of the event since it reveals how well-known performers like Abdul Wahab, Hijazi, and Um Kulthum were involved personally with events in Palestine.

Given the close friendship that joined the deceased with Isa'af al- Nashashibi, poet Ahmad Shawqi, and Mr. Muhammad Abdul Wahab, a friendship that had grown stronger after a number of private gatherings at al-Nashashibi's mansion, most of the audience was certain the concert would be canceled. But soon the curtains were drawn open and Mr. Abdul Wahab gave a brief speech, fraternally expressing his feeling of loss and offering his condolences to the Jarallah family and the people of Jerusalem. He then announced that he would not be canceling the concert, out of respect for art and for the audience, demonstrating his love and loyalty. And so, he started the performance looking visibly sad. But strangely, despite the great loss, he and his ensemble excelled in both singing and playing, having sensed the audience's thirst for his voice.[38]

THE *FLANEUR* AS PROTÉGÉ: BONDS WITH THE HUSSEINIS

With the establishment of a new independent Governership (*Mutasarraflik*) in Jerusalem in 1876, the status of Jerusalem's Husseini family was enhanced. The Husseinis went from being one of several leading families in the city to its most powerful clan, occupying the central institutions of local power in the Ottoman sultanate.

The Husseinis occupy the lion's share in the list of city notables in the Jawhariyyeh Albums, with many including biographical details that accompany the images. Rabah Effendi (d. 1886), the richest merchant in the city, became the *Naqib al-Ashraf*, the leading head of the syndicate of the local nobility. Tahir Effendi (1843–1908) was the chief Mufti, followed by his son Kamil, and after World War I, by Haj Amin.[39] Salim Husseini (d. 1908) became the Mayor, a position he held until 1897, when he was removed from office in favor of Yasin al-Khalidi. He remained, however, the main figure in the provincial representative council for the district (*majlis idarat al-Quds al-Sharif*). His sons Hussein Hashim (d. 1918) and Musa Kazhim (Kazim) Pasha al-Husseini became mayors, both before and after World

FIGURE 4.13. A young Wasif Jawhariyyeh leaning
on Mayor Salim al-Husseini. Athens Collection.

War I. Ismail al-Husseini (1860–1935?) was the progressive head of the Education Department in the late Ottoman period, establishing the first public school for girls. His villa in Sheikh Jarrah received Kaisar Wilhelm during his visit to the Holy Land in 1898, and later became the famous Orient House hotel. Finally, Said Bey al-Husseini (1878–1945) was an elected member of the Ottoman Parliament (*majlis al-mab'uthan*) after the constitutional (CUP) revolution of 1908, and chief censor of the press.[40]

Wasif's career as a musician and his engagement in public life were inextricably linked to his family connections to the Husseini families. Both his father, the lawyer Jiryis (Jirgis) Jawhariyyeh, and Wasif afterwards, depended on the Husseinis for securing public employment, mediating with the authorities when intercession and/or protection was needed (conscription, allocation of military service), and for their integration into the upper echelons of Jerusalem society. They both benefitted from these bonds in the provision of public employment and, in the case of Wasif, in the world of entertainment. Despite the discourse of intimacy and its egalitarian rhetoric, the relationship was essentially one of feudal patronage. Wasif knew where he stood with Mayor Hashim and his father, and Hashim Bey knew that he knew.

Throughout his diary, the narrative is permeated with references to the strong bonds that connected him and his family to the Husseinis. Those bonds begin with his father's service as a bailiff and tax collector for Salim Effendi al-Husseini (fig. 4.13). Later, Jiryis secured his membership in the Jerusalem Administrative Council (as Orthodox *mukhtar*) at the behest of Hussein Hashim. These services also included Jiryis's work as a lawyer in the Jerusalem's Circuit Court, and Wasif's first employment in the municipal animal services.

It was through his relationship with Haj Salim that Wasif's father established a bond that lasted for three generations. The Husseinis had acquired tax farming rights (known as *iltizam*) in the middle of the nineteenth century in the Jerusalem area—extending from Saris, Suba, Beit Naqubah, and Khirbat 'Amr in the western Jerusalem, all the way to 'Ain Sinya. In those villages, peasants paid their taxes to their landlords, from which the Husseinis extracted the *'ushr* (tithe) for the state treasury. Jirjis Jawhariyyeh, who was already the *mukhtar* of the Orthodox community in the Old City, was one of Haj Salim's main bailiffs in the collection of these taxes.[41] In Sheikh Jarrah, north of the Old City, Haj Salim set up a family diwan next to the family mansion. The diwan served as a guesthouse for ceremonial occasions, as well as a reception hall for clients and farmers of the Husseinis who had complaints and wanted Haj Salim to intercede on their behalf or settle their debts.[42] As the family businesses expanded, and the peasant claims increased, Husseini began to depend on the elder Jawhariyyeh to deal with those claims as well. In return for his services, Haj Salim secured him a position in Jerusalem's Shar'ia court—one of the few Christians to be appointed in this position.[43] Jurjis later became as a member of the city council, representing the Rum Orthodox *ta'ifah*.

When Hussein Effendi died in February of 1918, Wasif wrote an intimate tribute recalling his early indebtedness to "my second father". He recalls,

> In my early youth I used to accompany him during the summer months to the family estates in Khirbat Dayr 'Amr and to Beit Susin—as one of his sons. During those years he intervened for me to enroll in the Dusturiyahh school, run by *ustaz* Khalil Sakakini, and made sure that my fees were paid. Later he did the same by enrolling me at the Mutran school, where I continued to study until 1914, when the school closed during the war. . . . He gave me the earliest encouragement to study in my musical instrument and in my singing career. When he became mayor of Jerusalem I became his [personal] assistant, and his aide when he conducted business in Karak and the Dead Sea.[44]

When Hussein Effendi was dismissed from the mayorality during the war by Jamal Pasha, Wasif became his confidante, trusting him with his finances and private errands.

Occasionally Wasif flaunted this relationship by assuming an informal camaraderie with his patrons, as in a rare photograph of a young Wasif in his early twenties, in his *robe du chambre*, leaning on the fully attired dean of the Husseinis, the venerable Salim ibn Hussein al-Husseini (fig. 4.14). Wasif, at this time, was working closely as an assistant to his son, mayor Hussein Hashim. This picture is not included in any of the albums, but appears separately in the Athens collection. Wasif is leaning on the seated senior Husseini, affectionately holding his frail hand and gazing straight at the camera. A case of role reversal, although the pose is both intimate and filial. The viewer who is not aware of the relationship might think of the young man as the patron and Husseini as the patronized.

FIGURE 4.14. Hajj Salim al-Husseini, Head of Majlis Idarah, Jerusalem Council, 1901. Jawhariyyeh Album 1, IPS Beirut.

When Wasif came of age and finished his schooling, he maintained his close association with the Husseinis. He developed strong bonds with both sons of Haj Salim, Musa Kazhim Pasha and Hussein Hashim. The Husseinis, like the Khalidis, were pillars of the Ottoman regime, equally in the Hamidian period and after the constitutional revolution in 1908, which brought the CUP, the Young Turks, to power. They benefited from top appointments in the local administration, as well to judgeships and *qaimmakams*.

The Husseinis, in particular, were able to secure commissions in public enterprises such as the building of a seaport on the Dead Sea during the war. Several photographs showing Jamal Pasha visiting the Dead Sea installations in the company of Mayor Husseini appear in the Matson Collection in the Library of Congress. During Haj Salim's tenure as mayor (1887–97), he undertook a number of urban development schemes in the city, including the paving and expansion of the main internal roads of the city and the establishment of a public park, known as Manshiyyeh, next to City Hall.[45] He entrusted the supervision of garden to Jirjis Jawhariyyeh. Wasif recalls:

> The Park and its trees, plants, ponds, and the fountains were all designed by my father and extended, in the beginning, as far as the road to Sisters of Compassion. A base was placed over a well and covered with an engraved wood and tin rooftop, and wooden chairs were fixed around it for the members of the state's military band.[46]

The Manshiyyeh band performed on Fridays, Saturdays, and Sunday for the public (fig. 4.15). One of its lead musicians was the renowed Sheikh 'Umar al-Batsh from Aleppo, who later became Wasif's main oud teacher. After the death of Haj Salim, Wasif and his brother Khalil contracted the running of the Manshiyyeh

FIGURE 4.15. A musical performance in Jerusalem's Manshiyyeh Garden, Jaffa Street, 1903. Matson Collection, Library of Congress.

garden café from Salim's son, Hussein Hashim, who was by now also mayor. Wasif performed with his own band, singing and playing the oud, while Khalil helped with the light fare. He had brought with him gastronomic skills, including the serving of iced widgets with 'araq for the mezza. The Manshiyyeh Café competed with the Aristidi Bar, next door, which was run by a Greek who was, Wasif comments, "father of Miss Nina, the current mistress of Archbishop Epiphanius."[47]

Concubinage occupied a noticable space in the life of the Jerusalem aristocracy. Wasif goes to great lengths to distinguish between daughters, wives and the paramours of his patrons and the lives of sex workers during World War I. During these years, bordellos were established under government and army supervision in Jerusalem and Jaffa to cater for Ottoman army officers, as well as to Austrian and German soldiers who were stationed on the southern front. Ihsan Turjman refers to public celebrations in the city where sex workers were brought in to entertain officers at the Fourth Army Manzil at the Notre Dame building at the behest of Amiralai Rushan Bey and Ahmad Jamal Pasha.

> Cemal Pasha issued an order today in celebration of the anniversary of Sultan Mehmet Rashad V's ascension to the throne. A big party was being prepared at the Commissariat to be presided over by the two Cemals and Rushen (Rushan) Bey and other senior admirals and officers. We were ordered to extend electric lights and decorations in the Gardens of Notre Dame de France. To celebrate the anniversary, a number of notables and their ladies were invited to Notre Dame. An orchestra performed while liquor flowed. A number of Jerusalem prostitutes were also invited to entertain the officers. I was told that at least fifty well-known prostitutes were among the invitees. Each officer enjoyed the company of one or two ladies in the garden compound.[48]

FIGURE 4.16. "Women of pleasure," Jaffa,
c. 1914. Albert Kahn Museum, Paris.

Local women sex workers were also often invited to enhance parties in the bachelor apartments of the Jerusalem potentates, known as *odahs*, some of whom were singers and players in Wasif's own band.[49] A photographic record of these sex workers is available from the Albert Kahn collection. This includes a short film reel from a Beirut bordello, including military clients, and several outstanding color prints of Jaffa's "women of pleasure" smoking their arghillehs with the (male) brothel keeper (fig. 4.16).[50]

By contrast, this is how Jawhariyyeh introduces us to the Jerusalem courtesans: "For a long time the custom in the country, particularly in Jerusalem, was for the notables of the city's well known families, al-Husseini, al-Khalidi, al-Nashashibi, and others, to have a mistress, provide a home for her, and spend their leisure time with her."[51] Wasif introduces us to several Jerusalem concubines who played a major role in the city's political and social life, educated professionals combining entertainment and social skills with business acumen. Among these women were Lea Tannenbaum, the mistress of Jamal Pasha, who later married the well-known lawyer Abicarius; Miss Nina Aristidi, the mistress of Archbishop Epiphanious; Kyriaki, the Greek consort of Fahim Nusseibi; "Um Mansur," the Jewish mistress of Raghib Bey an-Nashashibi, who later became his wife; and the Albanian-Greek mistress of Hussein Effendi al-Husseini. The latter occupies several pages in the Jawhariyyeh memoirs:

> Her name was Persifon, and she was well-known in Jerusalemite society, particularly for her ravishing figure, stunning beauty, and elegant style. When she went to visit the Church of the Holy Sepulchre, people would say that the patriarch visited.

Hussein Effendi had brought her over from Istanbul, and she remained with him for over seventeen years. She learned Arabic and he granted her total freedom to go out and spend summers in Beit Susin, and particularly in Dayr 'Amr.

Later, Persifon was placed in charge of the Dayr 'Amr estates, where she specialized in distilling thyme oil and sold it for medicinal purposes. She played a major role in sponsoring Wasif's musical career, bringing musicians to train him while he taught her how to play the oud. When Hussein Effendi was elected mayor, Wasif's father prevailed on him to get married to the "honorable Fatima, daughter of Muhammad Tahir al-Khalidi," thereby ending his relationship to Persifon. Deserted by her patron in her later career, Persifon moved into the Jawhariyyeh household, finding solace with her younger protégé.[52] What stands out among these colorful and detailed accounts of the fascinating social lives of paramours, in contrast to the one-dimensional appearances of Jerusalem sex workers and the virtual absence of working class and peasant women, is that his albums lack any reference to either. While this particular chapter cannot go into depth regarding the complex social history of gender, sex work, and/or family and sexual relations, we do invite scholars to explore this gendered social history of late Ottoman and Mandate Palestine through radical feminist methodologies that have emerged from Arab and Southwest Asian scholars over the past three decades. While we gesture to this in chapter 3's introduction, it bears repeating that the glaring distinction between the visual narrative of his albums and the written narratives in his memoirs seems to us to be a critical place where this books ends but, hopefully, future scholarship on the central role of gender and sexuality in the social reproduction of Palestinian elite and new urban petit-bourgeoisie can begin.

THE MELANCHOLIC JOURNEY OF HUSSEIN HASHIM

In "Melancholy Objects" Sontag notes that early photographs set themselves up as "cultural and historic objects to establish distinct and ideological paradigms. . . . Photography's social distance . . . manifested at its earliest in the conflict between the bourgeois and the peasant." She suggests that the "earliest surreal photographs," from 1850s France, characterized by "concrete, particular, anecdotal . . . moments of lost time, of vanished customs . . . seem far more surreal to us now than any photograph rendered abstract and potetic by superimposition, underprinting, solarization, and the like."[53]

One of the most evocative image in the Jawhariyyeh albums introduces us to Hussein Hashim, son of Salim Effendi, holding a horse's rein and leading his carriage on a muddy road on the outskirts of the city (fig. 4.17). There is no caption and no date. Hussein Hashim al-Husseini was the last presiding Ottoman mayor of the city during the bitter war years and witnessed the fall of the city to the advancing troops of General Allenby. In Jawhariyyeh's album housed in the IPS in Beirut, this picture of the lonely Hussein Hashim driving despondently into an

FIGURE 4.17. Hussein Hashem and his carriage. Jawhariyyeh Album 1, IPS Beirut.

unknown future appears next to the famous image of the surrender of Jerusalem taken by Lars Larson, head of the American Colony Photographic Section. As the American Colony photograph suggests, he was one of three Ottoman officials to present the act of surrender to British officers on their approach to Jerusalem on December 9, 1917. The impression given by the order of presentation is that of a broken and defeated man, leaving his beloved city after the act of surrender. The two pictures are juxtaposed to convey a feeling of capitulation and abandonment, an impression which was forgotten in the euphoria of the end of the war and the illusion of liberation.

Jawhariyyeh, in his retrospective memoirs, which I will discuss below, created a divide between the war years and the prewar years. His nostalgic projections were surprisingly focused on the war years and the "three years of anarchy" following British occupation—which saw an abundant spectrum of musical activities and flaneurism. By contrast the prewar years, which include Hussein Hashim's lonely trek to Beit Susin, were seen as years of formative youth, and stability for the city.

But the juxtaposition in the Beirut album creates an illusion, induced by the order of the images' presentation. In the Athens collection, the two photographs are instead separated by a number of sequences. The horse carriage in the muddy road appears much earlier in the album, and here is clearly identified in Wasif's handwriting—"Hussein Hashim al-Husseini and his *Tuk* carriage on the road to Beit Susin, 1907" (fig. 4.18). The dating is ten years earlier than the surrender date. Beit Susin was one of the Husseini estate villages, and was periodically visited by family members to oversee the crops and collect revenue. While the sense of melancholy is evoked by the muddy road and the greyness of the wintery land-scape, the picture was taken, we now realize, when Hussein Bey was at the height

FIGURE 4.18. Hussein Hashim on the road to Beit Susin, 1907. Considered with the earlier date, the image now conveys a relaxed leisurely stroll with a single horse carriage, the *tuk*. Athens Collection.

of his prestige and power. He had won the mayoral race by a majority vote and had embarked on a project of modernization and renovation of the city's infrastructure, including the building of a modern sewage system.[54]

THE SURRENDER OF JERUSALEM: THE FARCICAL MOMENT AND A TRAGIC DECISION

Conflicting accounts surround the apparent climactic meeting between the British and Palestinians upon the surrender of Jerusalem on December 9, 1917 (fig. 4.20). The standard eyewitness account of Ottoman surrender, if there is such a thing, comes from the memoirs of Major Vivian Gilbert's *The Romance of the Last Crusade*.[55] Gilbert's account, simultaneously romantic and farcical, provides us with a caricature of Mayor Hussein Hashim, who is unnamed in this British version of the surrender. The focus of the account is Private Murch, a cook in Allenby's army camped near Lifta, who is in search of eggs for his Major's breakfast. The cook sent to fetch the eggs from Lifta encounters Mayor Husseini with his entourage, looking for the advanced troops to provide a peaceful transfer of authority. Here is the encounter as described by Gilbert, in the cook's cockney accent, some ten years later:

> 'Where is General Allah Nabi?' enquired the man in the red fez [Mayor Hussein].
> 'Anged if I know, mister,' answered the private. 'I want to surrender the city please.
> 'Ere are ze keys; it is yours!' went the stranger, producing a large bunch of keys and
> waving them before the bewildered Britisher, who now began to think he had fallen

amongst lunatics. 'I don't want yer city. I want some heggs for my hoficers!' yelled the disgusted cook.[56]

Three further attempts at surrendering the city (to General Watson, Major-General Shea, and finally to Allenby himself) are made by the mayor before Allenby marches into Bab al-Khalil on December 11. Mayor Husseini dies two weeks later of pneumonia. Gilbert notes: "I could not help thinking he must have caught cold standing exposed to the inclement weather whilst he handed over Jerusalem, first to the cook, then to the brigadier, then to the major-general, and finally to the commander-in-chief."[57]

Jawhariyyeh was also a witness to these momentous events. But he provides us with a substantially different account. In his memoirs, he lists the sequence of events that led to the collapse of the city's defenses. He cites a historic meeting that took place in the Mutran building (St. George) on Nablus Road on the eve of December 8. The meeting was attended by 'Izzat Bey, Governor of Jerusalem and the city's top administrator. In coordination with the German command the commander of the Ottoman forces, 'Ali Fu'ad, had sent a signal approving the surrender of the city. Among those attending were the commander of the city's police force and members of the administrative council: Abd al-Qadir al-'Alami, Ahmad Sharaf, and Ishaq al-Asali.[58] Wasif accompanied Hussein Hashim, who had been deposed from his duties as mayor by the notorious Ottoman Governor of Syria, Jamal Pasha. He reports the proceedings as follows:

> Final Meeting with Mutassarif 'Izzat Bey at Mutran School
> The Governor [Izzat Bey] spoke at length about the deteriorating situation in the country, and the need to deliver Jerusalem immediately. The following decisions were made:

> - To restore Hussein Bey al-Husseini as mayor of Jerusalem.
> - Grant Hussein Bey official dispensation to surrender the city, addressed as follows (in Turkish)

> ### TO THE ENGLISH FORCES

> *In the circumstances of your siege of the city, and given your heavy bombardment and our fear from the impact of this bombardment on the holy sites, we are compelled to surrender the city at the hands of Mayor Hussein Bey al-Husseini, expecting that you will preserve Jerusalem as we have preserved it for close to 500 years.*

> —(SIGNED) IZZAT, MUTASSARIF OF JERUSALEM, 8–9.12. 1333[59]

All ethnically Turkish civil administrators in the city, including those of Registry, the land administration, and the Werko, withdrew with the armed forces from the Sheikh Jarrah/Nablus Road on the night of December 8.[60] Mayor Husseini travelled the next morning with the commander of the police and city notables

FIGURE 4.19. The iconic picture of surrender included by Jawhariyyeh in the Athens Collection with a listing of names of the remaining members of the city's council. This same photograph is listed in the Matson Collection at the Library of Congress with no names attached to it.

to Sheikh Bader to deliver the act of surrender to the advancing British forces. Wasif included in his memoirs the iconic picture of the initial surrender, taken by Lewis Larson of the American Colony (fig. 4.19). Unlike the standard image preserved by the Library of Congress, Wasif marked this copy with the names of all the accompanying dignitaries from the city council and their retinue, including Ahmad Sharaf, the commissioner of police; Haj 'Abd al-Qadir al-'Alami, head of the mounted police force (*sawaris*); and Shams al-Din and Amin Tahbub, officers in the Jerusalem police force.[61] The white flag flown in Sheikh Bader was held by Salim Bey, the Lebanese driver of Jamal Pasha, which Wasif claims to have personally delivered to him.[62] Wasif disputes the British claim that this was "a chance encounter" with a private soldier in search of eggs. He notes that the location of the surrender was Sheikh Bader, scene of substantial fighting with the Jerusalem Ottoman garrison, while the purported search for eggs was in Lifta. Furthermore, he notes the presence of two armed officers in the picture, and not a single unarmed cook.[63]

The death of his benefactor and patron Hussein al-Husseini mere days after the act of surrender was a major blow to Wasif. In his album, he displays the last picture of the mayor, a broken man, attending the surrender ceremony on December 11 (fig. 4.20). He is seen standing next to a mounted General Watson, just before

FIGURE 4.20. Detail of first surrender of Jerusalem to the British—Mayor Husseini with City Councilor Hussein al-Asali and a British officer, wrongly identified as T.E. Lawrence by the original caption. Photo: Lewis Larson. Matson Collection, Library of Congress; Jawhariyyeh Album 2, IPS Beirut

the entry of Allenby to the Bab al-Khalil plaza. He stands looking deserted and despondent next to Ibrahim al-Husseini and Mitri Salamah, uncertain as to what the future holds. His death was a turning point for Wasif's career and the beginning of a new era for Jerusalem and Palestine.

CONCLUSION: THE FLANEUR'S ANTI-NOSTALGIC RECOLLECTIONS

Wasif Jawhariyyeh recomposed his memoirs in the early 1960s, when he was in his sixties, on the basis of his notebooks, and on notes and captions inscribed into his photographic collection going back to the beginning of the century. In few cases he used verbal recollections attributed to his father going back as far as 1845.[64] Paradoxically this would be a case where the photographic collection, and its annotation, constituted a major source for the written memoirs, and not vice versa—as would be expected. I believe this to be the case since the written captions and annotations for the photographic albums identify people and events with dates that are either contemporary to the events (1912, 1917, 1929, 1933, and so on) or go back to the 1950s, when he resumed his musical career. Another marker comes from inscriptions and dedications made on images and musical notes. Wasif's musical notebook, which contains the notations of Jerusalem music that was performed at the turn of the century, includes an opening dedication to "our beloved Sultan Abdul Hamid."[65]

A picture of Wasif taken in the late fifties shows the man on his sixtieth birthday, lying on a lawn in a silk 'abayah near the Beirut corniche with a mixed look of boredom and nostalgia. An aging dandy and traumatized flaneur. A visual register absent from the photo albums themselves, his flaneurism is recalled from the earlier days of his bachelorhood—before his marriage to Victoria, and before he became "gainfully" employed in the Registry.

The Ottoman era was coming to a close. Wasif was entering his adulthood, but not quite an age of reason. These were the years of bachelorhood, before he got married and settled down. He had been overwhelmed by what he called a 'period of total anarchy' in his life, ushered in by the death of his patron, the mayor of Jerusalem, Hussein Effendi al-Husseini. Living like a vagabond, sleeping all day and partying all night, had left him bereft, in a condition he describes as 'vagabondage.' When his mother complained about him coming home late at night, if at all, he retorted with the famous line, 'Man talaba al-'ula sahar al-layali' ('He who seeks glory, must toil the nights').[66]

There is no standardized Arabic term for flaneur. Literary uses include "*mutasakki*" (the wanderer) and "*su'luk*" (the vagabond). The ambivalence is related to the absence of an equivalent to the (mostly) Parisian figure, experiencing the crisis of modernity, who was described by Baudelaire and Benjamin. But Wasif and many of his associate musicians were really neither vagabonds nor wanderers, and the available Arabic terms do not fit them. The word *mutasakki'* carries both the aura of "aimless wandering" and parasitism—while *su'luk* conveys a meaning of underclass rebellion that is not part of Benjamin's usage. However, the term is useful when we do think about crises that modernity perpetually precipitates. Also, the term is useful in thinking about crisis, in understanding how alienation is inbuilt into the modern condition and only exacerbated and metabolized in other ways within the colonial context.

In this review of patronage and the photographic image I have focused on Wasif's obsession with the modernity of Jerusalem at turn of the century through a series of spectacles that he documented in his photographic albums. In a comment on Benjamin's conception of photography and the flaneur, Kirsten Seale captures the essential nostalgic feature of this relationship. "The flâneur's movement," she argues, "creates anachrony: he travels urban space, the space of modernity, but is forever looking to the past. He reverts to his memory of the city and rejects the self-enunciative authority of any technically reproduced image . . . yet the authority of this trajectory is challenged by photography's product: the photograph, a material memory which is only understood by looking away from the future, by reading retrospectively."[67]

The instances I have used to describe Wasif's deployment of the photographic image were focused on the transformation of the cityscape and its ceremonial processions (Nabi Musa, Sitna Mariam, the Saturday of Light)—all of which transcended their original religious content and became public syncretic celebrations. Wasif the flaneur as su'luk/vagabond was a keen observer of the traditional performative theater (the shadow play, *karagoz*, and its more primitive manifestations in *sunduq al-'ajab*, the wonderous "magic box"). The third instance was a spectacle of collapse—the events and savage imagery of the Great War (hangings, digging of trenches by *corvée* labour, and battle scenes). Paradoxically Wasif's gaze is directed at the events of the war years itself and not at the ceremonial processions of peacetime. During the war years and their aftermath, Wasif was able to survive army discipline and savagery through his wits and performative skills as a musician. As he served the Ottoman Navy as what he calls a "oud officer," we see the war itself almost as a series of joyous affairs. The famine years which devasted Syria through food shortages and locust attack were celebrated by Wasif's atypical musical contribution, the

Karshat song—his only surviving musical composition—that became "the national anthem of Palestine," as he puts it sarcastically. In one photograph of a Damascus hanging of deserting soldiers, he managed to insert himself as a spectator of a theatrical event (see fig. 4.3). The "years of anarchy" (1917–20)—following the British occupation of Palestine and before the onset of the British Mandate and the Balfour Declaration—were spectacular days of freedom, recorded both in his memories of the musical nights he arranged in the Old City and in Musrara, and in the photographic images he preserved for those liminal moments.[68]

5

Our Photography

Refusing the 1948 Partition of the Sensible

Stephen Sheehi

ORIENTALISM AS THEFT: REDISTRIBUTION OF THE SENSIBLE

The Orientalist photographic archive is a stolen archive. Orientalism itself is the theft of the photographic index. Innumerable images of the visual geographies of indigenous peoples are recast into a vision where only the colonizer sees and, if she even exists, the colonized is only to be seen. In the case of Palestine, this vision is coded by the overarching "Holy Land" narrative that is entwined with the creation of Zionism itself. Orientalism stole the visual landscape of Palestine long before the Zionists. This indexical theft then is related epistemologically to 1948.

The theft of the photographic index is the colonial condition of photography, which deterritorializes the index. This is a condition of colonialism itself, which involves not only an expropriation of land but of visual indices, geographies and histories. While this assertion and larger implications are explored elsewhere, examples of Orientalism as theft can be found readily. Whether an image of the Pyramids, a veiled woman, the Bosphorous, or a Maronite priest, every image from "the East" was coerced by and/or conscripted into an Orientalist and colonialist signification system that coded these indexes even within nationalist discourses and systems of representation (fig. 5.1).

Until recent decades, the "history of photography in the Middle East" has been circumscribed by the works and adventures of European photographers during colonial expansion in the region. Joseph-Philibert Girault, James Graham. and James Robertson to Francis Bedford, Auguste Salzmann, and the Maison Bonfils, not Arab and Armenian photographers, occupy the space of the progenitors of "Middle Eastern photography" (fig. 5.2). What is the effect when we realize that

FIGURE 5.1. The famous Khalidi Library in Jerusalem in Bab al-Silsilah. Jawhariyyeh Album 1, IPS Beirut.

FIGURE 5.2. The Port of Yaffa (Jaffa) during the Ottoman Period, 1868. Photo: Bonfils. Jawhariyyeh Album 7, IPS Beirut.

none of Wasif Jawhariyyeh's photographs are "originals" that he took? He himself only appears in three images out of more than eight hundred, and is not a central figure in any of them. Rather, many of the photographs are reproductions of images taken by expatriate and Orientalist photographers, as well as reproduced from news and colonial sources. While it would be inaccurate to reduce Bonfils and the American Colony solely to their Orientalist predilections and consumer base, it is impossible for us to dissociate Orientalism— ideologically, politically, and discursively—from their photographic production.[1] They extracted and accumulated value from Palestine without compensation to or collaboration with the subjects (and objects) of their production. In order to understand the full force and potentiality of Wasif Jawhariyyeh's albums, we must make the basic but previously hidden methodological observation that *photography is a colonial mode of extraction, a mode of theft, a mode of theft facilitated by colonialism and colonial capitalism.* With Jawhariyyeh's collection in mind, this observation ponders what is produced through the adjacency of Orientalist and colonialist images in Jawhariyyeh's albums alongside indigenously-produced and circulated images. What is produced when these images, sitting side by side, one perhaps obfuscating the social origins of the other, coalesce into a Palestinian photographic archive?

The Jawhariyyeh albums expose a number of examples that demonstrate how Orientalism is a form of theft. Since the Holy Land discourse enframes so much of the representation of Palestine, let us look at one very non-Biblical example from the Jawhariyyeh Collection that simply and unambiguously illustrates how Orientalism is a form of indexical appropriation. Let us see how material realities, the lifeworlds, and living social relations are displaced by Orientalized generic codes that commodify an image for colonial power and exchange. The image of the exterior of the Khalidi Library is one of the few photographs that appears twice in Jawhariyyeh's albums. It is a well-known image of five *'ulema* standing in front of the door and, in the "original" postcard, two men with mustaches, suits, and tarbushes (pl. *tarabish*) stand in the shadow of the doorway (fig. 5.1). The American Colony produced and commercially sold this photograph, titling it "Moslim Sheiks and Effendis" with a translation in German. (The adjacent French translation, "Biblioteque Khalidieh," matches the French and Arabic sign above the Library's door.) Jawhariyyeh, however, writes "The famous Khalidi Library in Jerusalem, in Bad al-Silsilah neighborhood" (fig. 5.3). The image could be the basis for a painting by Ludwig Deutsch, an Austrian Orientalist who frequently painted Muslim scholars and *'ulema.* The Orientalist photograph is ahistorical, invoking exoticized, sacred knowledge of the Islamic Golden Age. These "Moslim Sheiks and Effendis" and their ancient library could be from any time in the Islamic past. The coding of the English/German title only contributes to this sense of the timeless Muslim scholar, who inhabits no country other than *Dar al-Islam,* and who is now arcane in the modern moment.

The material and indexical reality of this image is displaced. In other words, the image is presented in a way that does not represent how Palestinian Arabs might

FIGURE 5.3. Top left: al-Hajj Muhammad Sa'id al-Shawwa; top right, Khalidi Library, 1900 (interior); bottom right: Khalidi Library. Jawhariyyeh Album 3, IPS Beirut.

have read this image. This is a reality of which Jawhariyyeh was well aware. The Khalidi Library was not an ancient repository for Islamic learning. It was, in fact, quite a modern creation, one of its time, and an enterprise that arose very much as a part of the *nahdah* ("enlightenment") project in the Arab world, particularly, in this instance, in Palestine. Founded in 1899 by al-Hajj Raghib al-Khalidi, scion of a powerful Jerusalemite family, the library was intended to be a public facility, housing the Khalidis' formable collection. Tahir al-Jaza'iri, the famous Islamic *salafi* reformer who had founded the illustrious Zawhariyah Library in Damascus, assisted al-Hajj as a part of opening a series of libraries throughout Bilad al-Sham. The Jerusalem library, Rashid Khalidi notes, was meant to "help restore the Arabs to prosperity by fostering knowledge, and enabling them to match the powerful cultural establishments created by foreign powers all over the region."[2] What distinguished the Khalidi Library from the venerable twelfth-century al-Maktabah al-Budayriyah, or the Aqsa Library on the grounds of al-Haram al-Sharif, was that its holdings "show both continued copying of earlier (classical) manuscript and the production of new religious and other texts in manuscript form late into the nineteenth century."[3] Equally relevant is that these canonical classical and contemporary Muslim manuscripts and scholarly works stood side by side in the library with the contemporary, cutting edge, *nahdah* journals of the day from Istanbul,

Beirut, Damascus, and Cairo, including *al-Jinan, al-Muqtataf, al-Jawa'ib* and *al-Manar*.⁴

The photograph was, in fact, taken upon the opening of the Library, and al-Hajj Raghib and Tahir al-Jaza'iri are among those standing in front of the doorway, along with Musa Shafiq al-Khalidi, Khalil al-Khalidi, and Muhammad al-Habbal of Beirut.⁵ These important figures also appear, sitting in the library, in another photograph in the album, while another copy of the exterior of the library is placed below it (fig. 5.3). Jawhariyyeh's choice and placement of images (exterior, interior, and prominent figures) depicts not a static, moribund space of the past or Orientalized "scholars" of outmoded "Islamic knowledge." Rather, the interplay of photographs, surrounded by images of leaders such as al-Hajj Sa'id al-Shawwa—mayor of Gaza City, member of the Supreme Muslim Council, and the Gaza representative to the Palestinian National Congress—clearly alert us to a dialogic narrative being established.

The apparatus and infrastructure of Orientalism (from the lens to the photography market to the scholarly book which might reproduce the image) erase the social value, codes, and meaning of these images. The purpose of Orientalism is to establish power, domination and an epistemological order of the world with a particular place for Arabs and Muslims and another place for Europeans, as Edward Said teaches us. This process occurs through the multiple apparatuses of Orientalism, photography being just one of many. This apparatus, as one piece of colonial infrastructure, *steals* the index from its context and transfers the value of the image into the colonial marketplace and into the imperial political arena. This process needs to be made apparent in Palestine, where colonial, imperialist, and Zionist powers have sought to erase the theft of land and displacement of its people. Therefore, notable Arab intellectuals with deep social networks that connect Jerusalem to Beirut to Damascus are hollowed out and recoded to be legible to the colonizer but also in order to delegitimize any possible challenge to colonial rule. These are the mechanics of Orientalism, where representation of *generic* Arab subjects becomes evidence of the vestiges of a noble but now archaic Islamic clergy, rattling around in a dilapidated Oriental city that needed to be reclaimed for Christianity. (It should not be forgotten that, for all their sympathies for the "native," the American Colony was a Protestant missionary project.) The colonizer's vision mediates the reception and reading of the photograph of the Khalidi Library, its very name obstructed by the cliché English/German title. Orientalism pushed al-Hajj Raghib out of the frame and replaced him with a timeless, typecast "Moslem sheikh."

By lingering in Wasif Jawhariyyeh's photography albums, this chapter offers a radical method for confronting the lasting apparatuses and infrastructures of colonial modernity, which includes the settler-colonization of Palestine. To think about this method as an anti-colonialist as well as decolonialist method, Amílcar Cabral's words seem to reach across continents and time. In speaking of colonialism, Cabral tells us, "When imperialism arrived in Guinea it made us leave our history—*our history.*"[6] The sentiment must be extended to the study of photography, considering the central and unique role the visual plays in the history of the colonized. This is so not only in constructing or manifesting representation itself, as Edward Said masterfully taught us, but also as, quite literally, illustrating that which is to be seized, controlled, dominated, and exploited by the colonial rulers.

If imperialism evicts us from "our history," I offer in this chapter a means to consider Jawhariyyeh's albums as a version of *our photography*—Palestinian Arab photography. In doing so, these albums allow us claim "our history," as Palestinians and as Arabs. The composition and reintroduction of these images into circulation among Palestinians and non-Palestinians present us with start of a radical *process*; to reappropriate photography as space (visual, representational, geographic and physical) and to repatriate Palestinians from that land and to evict colonizers. This is not metaphor but a suggested method to approach extractive Orientalist photography. The process is not determined by me as a militant Lebanese Arab, or even by we three authors. It is determined by the Palestinian people. Yet, here, we present only one additional impetus for this process that has been initiated by Palestinians since 1947. Therefore, I start this chapter with alerting us to photography as one apparatus of Orientalism and colonialism, by alerting us to theft, not as a crime around the sanctity of property, but as a *violation of the relationship between people and their social relations to others, places and objects.* Photography played a central role in Orientalism's grand heist of the index. Jawharriyyeh's collection of that heritage, intentionally or unintentionally, reframes this theft within the context of the index's hereditary proprietors, the Arab inhabitants of Palestine; that is, Palestinians.

Photography, as an apparatus of colonialism, provided the visual raw material for Orientalism's visual and discursive organizing of the "East" and the "Holy Land." Moreover, it facilitated colonialism's "distribution of the sensible," or, I should say, appropriation and redistribution of the sensible. In this chapter, I will borrow tactically from Jacques Rancière but also I will discuss how we can do this while building a decolonial methodology to think about photography in connection with living social relations of the colonized. But for now, I point to how Rancière explains that the "distribution of the sensible" structures how particular forms of the senses, in particular visuality and aesthetics, are "perceived and thought of . . . as forms that inscribe a sense of community."[7] While we might understand this as a means of subaltern struggling to forge out communal spaces, solidarities, and realities, we must recognize how those forms of thinking about the "native" and colonized self, even in terms of colonial "resistance," were informed by a radical epistemological shift that Arab intellectuals and reformists retooled for their own subject and social formation (as is seen in the example of the Khalidi Library).

Throughout this chapter, I choose to push upon the limitations and full implications of the language of a number of French theorists whose thought aims to critically, even radically, disrupt predominant thinking about the visual and the philosophy and politics of aesthetics, art, photography, and performance. I will briefly touch on the ethics, tactical relevance and circumscribed limitations of using high "French theory" to think in decolonial terms. Such a digression is important when we continue to debate within decolonial and postcolonial studies the relevance and place for "Western theory" in the struggle for anti-colonial, anti-white supremist and anti-capitalist liberation. That is, despite their upending of hegemonic methods and theories of art, aesthetics, and social action, many of these thinkers, despite their theoretically left politics, remain incredibly "white" and disconnected from issues of race and colonialism. More specifically, they are shockingly equivocal regarding the rights of the Palestinian people in the face of Zionist settler colonialism, Israeli apartheid, and human rights violations. In the case of Rancière, who has expressed sympathy for Palestinians' human rights, I focus on his "aesthetic theory" because the limitations of his language within his powerful theorization direct our analysis to the structural creases and telling-ironies in the logic of sensibility that he could not perceive, in ways that the original theory actually might otherwise foreclose.

For example, in speaking about his "distribution of the sensible," Rancière's "distribution" is *partage*, partition, or, perhaps even worse, "sharing." The implications and resonance of the term "partition" is hardly innocent in the context of Palestine and in the Arab world. Similarly, it has powerful meaning and implications in India and Pakistan, Ireland and occupied Northern Ireland, Cyprus, the Koreas, and Vietnam. The full, global, and Southern implication of *partage* seems otherwise undetectable to Rancière. If photography "distributed" or partitioned the sensible in the colonial context, it also *partitioned off visual geographies* and lifeworlds. This partitioning aimed to ethnically cleanse them from the visual fields and forge master Orientalist and colonialist narratives. These narratives live on in pernicious and violent afterlives. It is within these partitioned visual geographies that the colonized are interpolated by colonial power and modernity, where they are conscripted or coerced to represent themselves, and to seek and produce meaning. Therefore, the colonized native reproduces or pushes back on partitioning of community and history, on the redistribution of the sensible that positions the oppressed as inconvenient or exotic features within a stolen land and history commandeered by the colonizer.

Jawhariyyeh's albums reclaim not only stolen images but the stolen index—visual and cultural references that are given meaning through social relations of the origins and their "context." In reclaiming this index, Jawharriyeh, we will see, "redistributes" them, returning them to their proper space and time of Palestinian history and visual geography. This is not to assert that Jawhariyyeh's Palestinian vision is so exclusive that it shares no overlap with colonial or even Zionist vision. Jawhariyyeh's collecting practices were clearly informed by Orientalism. Furthermore, his *nahdah* perspective was structured by the civilizational discourses and cosmopolitanism of Arab modernity. These are the same discourses that compelled al-Hajj Raghib al-Khalidi, who was fascinated by European positivist social paradigms, to establish a library that would "help to civilize the country, move forward its affairs, and raise up its people, who are ignorant of Palestine's virtues, although others appreciated them."[8] But also within this civilizational worldview, al-Hajj Raghib realized how Europe's appreciation of knowledge, both secular and Islamic, produced, in his words, their "wealth, happiness, and greed for what belongs to other lands."[9] In other words, Jawharriyeh is not "returning" to some authentic meaning but producing knowledge and meaning within the context of Mandate Palestine.

We should not romanticize Jawhariyyeh's albums as a explicitly "alternative view" or intentional "counter-visuality" that consciously attacks Orientalist representation.[10] The matrix of modernity presents the multitemporal "problem-space," which "conscripts," as David Scott might say, Jawhariyyeh to receive, organize, and find value and meaning in photographs within particular political and civilizational paradigms.[11] In the case of Wasif, this modality was intimate with Arab modernity. Therefore, I propose that we understand Jawhariyyeh's albums, which partially were organized and composed after *al-Nakba*, as a refusal of the 1948 partition of the sensible.[12] While Jawhariyyeh subscribed to *nahdah* civilizational discourses, which simultaneously challenged and reinscribed Orientalist authority, the deployment of the images served a pointed goal and emanated a particular effect.

That is, the images that Wasif deploys were "snatched" not only from history but from Zionist and colonialist history, snatched through the apparatuses of Orientalism. They are surviving images. The "surviving image," according to Georges Didi-Huberman, "always describes another time and thus it *disorients* history and opens it up, making it more complex."[13] This disorienting history, as offered by this chapter, is the result of exposing how objects are meaningful in ways that are not immediately apparent because they are entangled in the "heterochronies" of present.[14] They are enmeshed in knots of the past(s) and present. Every image in Jawhariyyeh's albums is circumscribed by these synchronous heterochronies, the expressed coterminous temporalities of the late Ottoman and Mandate eras and of post-1948 Palestine. Therefore, it is a mistake to see Jawhariyyeh's photographs as artifacts of the past alone or as a nostalgic testimony to lost Palestinian lifeworlds "before the Diaspora."

But, the photographs are "surviving images" in ways that strip Didi-Huberman's theory of the limitations of its own linguistic, social, and, yes, ideological origins. "Disorient" and "survival," like *partage*, take on additional meaning within the context of Palestine and the Arab world. We have seen how Jawhariyyeh's albums might "disorient" Orientalism's grand move of theft. However, more central to the historical, social, and political impact of Jawhariyyeh's photographic project, "survival" signifies something absent in Didi-Huberman's use of *nachleben*, namely the politics and presence of the colonized. Jawhariyyeh's albums "dis-orient," un-orient, Palestinian history. The images of Jerusalem, its communal members, its cityscapes, its religious rituals and festivals, its civil society, and its politics, are not exclusively coded by Orientalist indices, nor do they hold pretensions to nativist authenticity and purity. Jahwariyyeh repurposed a slew of images, including Orientalist images, that serve not to "haunt" but to *refuse* to become a specter of the past. They refuse to go away just because one is stateless. They are the kernel of reality and history that infuses the present moment. If Palestinian experience is latent in these images, it is only so in the mind and tradition of colonialism, Zionism, and Orientalism. As we will discuss in depth, these images in the viewfinder of the Palestinian "spectator" are imbricated in an unbroken past-present-future continuum of social reality: Palestine.

The emphasis on Jawhariyyeh's albums as "surviving images," an expression of persistence, perseverance, and refusal that speaks across temporalities, is not rhetorical analysis. It is the assertion that the "surviving images" are not abstract but social facts. Jawhariyyeh's photographic albums are not a gesture of historical memory, an academic exercise, or a nostalgic enterprise. His Palestinian photographic archive is not a rectification of history, a rewriting of Palestinian history into History, or a reintroduction into the field of photographic visuality. Rather, Jawhariyyeh's albums "disorient" history and refuse European and Zionist histories that have tried unsuccessfully to imagine them out of History and, indeed, out of the photographic archive and out of their land. Jawhariyyeh's albums redistribute the sensible, rejecting the partition and the displacement of the Palestinians out of the visual geographies of the Orient that started with Orientalism's theft and continue through colonialism until today.

THE PALESTINIAN LIVING BODY OF PHOTOGRAPHY

In the previous chapters, Issam Nassar and Salim Tamari have provided us with a social, cultural and, indeed, personal history of Wasif Jawhariyyeh's seven photography albums, titled *Tarikh Filastin al-musawwar* (*The Illustrated History of Palestine*) and their annotated index. They have shown how this work was a part of what Nassar identifies as a self-generated archive that included an extensive written chronicle of his life, a number of personal and miscellaneous photographs, cultural artifacts, instruments, and sheet music.[15] In this chapter, I have begun with a discussion of how we must not dismiss but radically re-appropriate the extracted value from Orientalist photography. In doing so, we may dwell within the localized, contextual, indigenous historical spaces which Jawhariyyeh himself has set out for us.

Jawhariyyeh was a bureaucrat, a fixer, a "flaneur," a husband, a son, a stepson, a loyal subject of elite families, a musician, a collector, an Ottoman, a Palestinian, a Jerusalemite, a Christian Arab. All of these subject positions, we will see, are connected to a social network, a social space, an urban and rural landscape, a cultural tapestry, and political hierarchy, all of which exist in Palestine, and more specifically, in its historic and eternal capital Jerusalem. The social, the political, the cultural, and the personal space opened up in these albums by Jawhariyyeh, and contours given by Nassar and Tamari, permit us to consider and acknowledge the "visibility" of Palestine and the Palestinian both in, out, before, and beyond the photographic archive. Concretizing how the Palestinian appears, how the Palestinian becomes recognizable, and that the Palestinian Arab subject is a *social fact* is central to this book and, unfortunately, remains a necessity considering that Zionism has worked assiduously to make it *invisible*, a condition of Zionist settler colonialism on which scholars have focused in recent years.[16]

Yet one of these scholars, Nadera Shalhoub-Kevorkian, also points us to the "livability" of Palestinian existence, the ethos of Palestinian life as organically connected to space and place throughout historic Palestine that defies sustained settler colonial violence.[17] Centering Palestinian life compels us to deliberate the number of dimensions within the "visibility" of the Palestinian subject when we speak of photography, if not contemporary Palestine itself. The mere mention of Palestine brings to the surface the contradiction within "visibility" and photography—namely, who has the right to be seen? Who has the right to be acknowledged? Whose visibility is weighed over others?[18] The photographic archive is often deployed to give value to the Palestinian subject erased and displaced through Zionist settler colonial history-making.[19] But such a gesture forces us to argue "for" Palestinian value always in relationship to the value of the Zionist settler and settler state.

In order to refuse photography's invitation to prove or disprove the value of Palestinian life and present as well as historical claims to Palestine through a discussion, I would like to adopt a "queer phenomenology" of the Palestinian object of photography, to play on Sara Ahmed's work.[20] In other words, rather than searching for the emergence of a Palestinian object in the photographic archive, I assume the "living body" of the Palestinian, as Ahmed would say in making Edmund Husserl relevant to us. This living body of the Palestinian is, we will see, both a current and historical fact, to be understood as the constant, as a social fact, rather than the variable in the equation of thinking about the photography of Palestine. The "queer picture on the table," then, is the photograph of Palestinian bodies, spaces, families, collectives, genders, sexualities, classes, object, artifacts, lands, cities, and towns, all in synchronic (even at times antagonistic) relationship with one another.[21]

Therefore, this chapter approaches the "Palestinian object" of the photograph as an agentic subject. This subject of photography is representative of the living body (social and corporeal, individual and collective) of the Palestinians, that is, the "emancipated" Palestinian spectator within and outside the Palestinian archive and the social history of Jerusalem that Nassar and Tamari describe, respectively. The concept of the "emancipated" Palestinian spectator is borrowed from Jacques

Rancière. With some adjustment, the concept allows us to think of the living body of the Palestinian as a subject of history and a subject of the land, who may "look through" and "look at," as Geoffrey Batchen says, the Palestinian photograph.[22] But in keeping with Ahmed's queer methodologies, the concept of the "emancipated Palestinian spectator" permits us to see the Palestinian subjects of the image also looking back at themselves into the future from within the image itself, reaching across and connecting history, the present, and the certainties of a liberated future.

Before proceeding further, it is essential to acknowledge but avoid the threat of ableist metaphors and language when one relies on terms such as "seeing" or "visible" or even "spectator," even within the study of visual culture and social history.[23] The idea of a "spectator," as Rancière reminds us, is traditionally coded as the "opposite of knowing" and "of acting," alerting us to the ableist association of sight with awareness, intelligence, and consciousness. Yet, pursuing Rancière's observation with this in mind, "seeing" and "visibility" should be disconnected from the "ability" or "disability" of biological functions of sight. Rather, I think of them as modes of controlling what is assumed to be known, knowable, what is already "coherent," legible and, hence, permissible. This conceptualization of "seeing" and "visibility" works against defining knowledge through the physical process of vision/sight, just as Rancière's use of "spectator" upends the understanding of the active actor and passive "viewer." Rather than a capricious or irresponsible choice of words, I see the inversion of the role of the emancipated spectator as a clear parallel to how Palestinian subjects are "viewed" or removed from the tableau of "sight" that constitutes knowledge. They are "seen" or not as "victims," as subjects or objects of knowledge, either worthy or unworthy of empathy.

"Spectator," however, in the context of this chapter, as with Ahmed's living body, alerts us to how those indigenous subjects are posed as subjects to be looked at within the photograph (bound by the production of the photograph). It also marks how this one-directional viewing produces social meaning and value, rather than understanding how multiple vectors between these subjects create value and meaning. This meaning and value, produced through the social relations of subjects in and out of the photograph, which include the object's circulation and display, all function within the social relations of the Palestinian community. The theft of this value, "the visual evidence" of the theft itself, by colonialism and Zionism may be reminiscent in some way of the theft of the relationship between labor and its product by the ruling capitalist class, inasmuch as they share the crucial role that invisibility (and mystification) plays within systems of extraction.[24]

To put it more simply, this chapter seeks to learn from Palestinian spectators qua subjects, like Wasif and those in his community, who are located both in and looking at the photograph, in order to produce social meaning that undermines the force and violence of settler colonialism. The spectator is not an onlooker. The Palestinian spectator is agentic while also structured by the contradictions, competing desires, and conflicts of any subject of Arab modernity. In this regard, Jawhariyyeh's photographic albums offer us an opportunity to encounter a transhistorical Palestinian spectator, not a displaced subject of history whose relationship to the photograph as historical testimonial remains nostalgic and passive. Instead, his albums present us with an example of how the Palestinian subject qua spectator's relationship with photography, her own sense of dominant visuality and history, is generative of a sustained, coherent, and material Palestinian identity.

Against the social, urban, and biographical histories that Tamari and Nassar have given us, I further explore the ways in which we can start to "unfix," as Jennifer Bajorek suggests, the coloniality of how we engage the photography of Palestine and the Arab world.[25] Jawhariyyeh's albums challenge us to define "Palestinian photography" not as derivative of "Western" photographic practices. They challenge us to "uproot Western knowledge from its central place" in our analytic of those albums, while, at the same time, understanding how Wasif himself might have been saturated by those forms of modern knowledge production as a subject of Arab modernity.[26] While I gestured to Ahmed's queer phenomenology, this chapter, unfortunately, cannot offer a comprehensive method and philosophy of decolonizing photography. The albums do offer us, however, an opportunity to explore, in Ahmed's words, "multiple forms of contact between others," and between the living and dead bodies of Palestinians selves, I would add.[27] The "double critique" emerges as a mode of thinking about how Palestinian modern subjects have negotiated positions that have always been subject to dissonant social and ideological forces. Or in other words, Jawhariyyeh's albums provide us with an opportunity to parse out a political and social history of Palestinian selfhood, not only of consensus but *dissensus*, to further borrow from Rancière.[28] Such a *dissensual* history of contradictions and polarities allows us to represent Palestine as more than a nation of victims, a nation of loss, and an irretrievable historic (rather than contemporary) nation. It also allows us to understand Palestinian identity as a part of larger Arab identity intersecting with sectarian forces, the forces of the local ruling class, their own antagonisms and alliances with the imperial center, and so forth.

My use of the concepts of "dissensual" history and "emancipated spectator," or any other theoretical language, should not be seen as gratuitous, obfuscating, or a means of recentering Eurocentric thinking about the non-West. Indeed, I have always been struck by how Palestinian identity has been held to a level of coherence and consistency in ways that no other national identity is; how Palestinians have to prove they called themselves this or that before 1920 or 1948; how Palestinians have to have lived in the same house for generations because if their families had emigrated to a village from Lebanon or Jordan in the nineteenth century, then clearly they have no right to their land or their identity. Therefore, by using dissensus, for example, I want to license scholarship to platform difference and contradictions as constitutive of identity as much as the nationalist myths of similarity and sameness. Even though the term originates from Rancière, I mobilize it, with great deliberation as a Lebanese Arab scholar, within decolonial methodologies as set out by generations of anti-colonial scholars.[29] I seek to strategically parse photography as a historical and visual source that is structured by synergies, but also by contradictions and tensions that might not need always to be reconciled. In fact, co-existing tensions are essential to the production of knowledge that liberates suppressed, repressed, and displaced histories.

Approaching Jawhariyyeh's photographic montage as *dissensus* reveals the albums as a coming-together of the many different lived worlds and temporalities that co-exist in tension. In other words, Jawhariyyeh's albums must first and most obviously be understood as an assertion of transhistorical Palestinian national identity, but one that should not be romanticized but understood as dynamic and conflictual. Jawhariyyeh's deployment and arrangement of photographs represent the social relations and politic history of Jerusalem and, to a larger extent, Palestine. In doing this, the photographic oeuvre undertakes, by default, a process of undoing, reworking the Orientalist and colonial visual narratives that erase Palestinians from the imaginary of Holy Land and the state now known as Israel. Against a sustained tension with the legacies of colonial representation, Jawhariyyeh also presents, in quite high resolution, the visuality of an ossified political class that miscalculated resistance to British colonial authority and Zionist settlement, as much as he presents a Palestinian reality of a communal order that has been sustained even to the present.

THEORY AS A WEAPON

Cobbling together a methodology and theoretical apparatus for looking at Palestinian photography is a dynamic struggle of navigating between the hegemony of modern forms of European thought (including colonial logics of identity, governance, and *homo economicus*), Arab modernity, and the anticolonial struggle. In navigating this tension, I employ theorists from the Arab world, the Global South, and Europe. I do so not in order to make the Palestinian worthy of theoretical discussion or out of a requirement to make this study relevant to the academy at large. As a scholar who has critically engaged the intellectual, material and visual history of the Arab world for years, I have always felt coerced, when it came to Palestine, to suspend a critical theoretical apparatus, because the most fundamental historical and material realities of Palestine are negated as a matter of "fact" within the mainstream. To ponder, for example, how the contradictions of capitalism structured the reformation of a Palestinian ruling class before 1948 or how Palestinian Arabs were involved in "constructing" their own "imagined" community seemed irresponsible when we are busy with the relentless struggle to oppose the mainstreaming and, indeed, institutionalizing (including within legal systems) of constitutive Zionist settler colonial myths that include "Palestine was a land without a people" and that "there is no such thing as Palestinians."

Perhaps much later than I should have, I have come to realize that this coercion (prohibiting the use of theory) is, in fact, the effect of the "coloniality of knowledge" that structures the politics of inquiry around Palestine within the academy and political organizing. The suspension of the "applicability" of theory is crucial to perpetuating positivist, Orientalist, Zionist, and neocolonial developmentalist discourses about the Arab world. Yet these discourses are reiterated themselves by Arab intellectuals, who themselves are often caught in the binaries of a colonialist epistemology that predispose their engagement with neoliberal empire and its regional and Zionist allies. As a graduate student in 1990s Beirut, I was specifically told that Palestine "is not ready for 'deconstruction.' We can't afford it. We are still trying to get our country back and you want 'deconstruct' it!?"

The Arab intellectual who told me this was not wrong. While he himself was an admirer of European political philosophy, he, as a Palestinian in exile, rightfully suspected the ways that Western theory displaces indigenous subjects, corralling them into realms of abstraction.[30] But the epistemological framing of scholarship around Palestine that occludes critical theoretical approaches has another effect. It functions to steal the "weapon of theory," as Amílcar Cabral says, from the hands of the anticolonial *indigènes*.[31] Cabral wants instead to liberate "theory" from its colonial, racist, Eurocentric origins and seize it as a means to dismantle the epistemological and economic systems from which European theory emerges (and, indeed, itself critiques). Cabral guides us, in that our mobilization of indigenous and non-indigenous forms of theory, as Arabs and subjects of coloniality and racial capitalism, allows us to critically approach the "presuppositions and objectives of national liberation in relation to social structure" in the service of maintaining the continuity of a "revolutionary consciousness" at the heart of Palestinian existence and resistance.[32]

For this reason, I approach Rancière's concepts of "dissensus" and "spectator" with particular caution and weariness, contemplating what they might obfuscate as much as illuminate, because his analysis is very much limited to a structural relationship between actors, viewers, and the stage of European theatre. To me they are helpful terms to amplify the process of making the illegible legible and the suppressed perceivable. But also, the shortcomings and inabilities of Rancière's theory (as well as those of Maurice Merleau-Ponty and Georges Didi-Huberman, whose diminishment of Palestinian life is decriable and indefensible) must be noted not out of pedantic criticism of their Eurocentrism. Rather, as scholars always engaged in the dialectics of decolonial thinking, we also understand the blockages, limitations, and shortcomings of their thinking and theorizing as actually symptomatic of the systems of coloniality, colonial power, and racial authority that authorize settler colonialism.

In other words, the theoretical language of "French theory," for me, helps betray the processes of settler-colonial extraction that lay at the foundation of how we approach "Arab photography. For example, Rancière's concept of "spectator" is consciously and strategically repurposed in this study of Palestinian visuality to "challenge the opposition between viewing and acting," understanding that "viewing is also an action that confirms or transforms" the relationship of subjects in relations to "structures of domination and subjection."[33] I therefore critically and tactically deploy the work of a small handful of European theorists very consciously in orbit with anticolonial and decolonial thinkers from the Global South and Palestinian and Arab scholars in Southwest Asia, Europe and the country now known as the United States. In doing so, I am working to procure a method, albeit imperfectly, of undoing colonial, Zionist, and capitalist hegemony that relies on making the invisible visible, whether that is the erasure of black and indigenous people or women and labor from social production and surplus value. Thinking about the Palestinian subject as Palestinian spectator takes a step in this methodological direction. It acknowledges the collective social value of image and knowledge production that continues to be produced *communally* by Palestinians, both under apartheid or in forced exile, as Jawharriyeh himself lived after 1948.

ARAB MODERNITY: SHOULD WE *READ* JAWHARIYYEH'S PHOTOGRAPHY ALBUMS?

Let us then begin to reapproach Jawhariyyeh's photographic albums with a renewed decolonial perspective, one that not only embraces a "disorientation" of histories otherwise based on theft and dispossession but an approach that begins from the primacy of the life and presence of the Palestinian people. To answer the fundamental question as to how to read Jawhariyyeh's albums, we must locate them with in two fundamentally separate, but overlapping, fields of inquiry, Palestine and photography. In answering what do these photographs mean, we may consider the enunciative *function* of the albums; that is, they testify to the presence of Palestine that cuts across and compresses time.[34] Considering the assortment of genres and photographers that populate Wasif's albums, the gambit of photographs—notably the reliance on expatriate and European alongside native photographers to narrate an indigenous history—presents a challenge to those who are seeking a truly "authentic" Palestinian "viewpoint." This leads to the perennial tension in using the photographic archive to explore historical realities. Therefore, in seeking a method for reclaiming "our photography" in the Orientalized archive, it is important to squarely identify photography as the medium that mediates the relationship between Jawhariyyeh as auteur, the Palestinian subject (or, as we will see, spectator), and Palestine as a social and political fact.

To undervalue Jawhariyyeh's choice of photography as a medium of history-telling or to unproblematically view photography as a "window to the past" prevents us from exploring how the mode of visuality (i.e., the way Jawhariyyeh sees his society, how he as a Palestinian subject envisions history, and how he visually organizes his narrative) is historically and ideologically produced in and by Arab modernity in the late Ottoman and Mandate period. Contrarily, interpreting the photograph as solely an ideologically overdetermined discursive act with no material reality overlooks photography's assumed quality to provide a visualization of empirical historical realities. Therefore, situating the history of photography in Palestine disassembles the structural binaries that delineate the trite discussion of the photograph as either pure document or pure artifices or a purely "Western" product of seeing versus an "alternate" gaze of the colonized, as Ali Behdad teaches us.[35]

Even if Orientalist and colonialist photographic tropes and representation often mediated indigenous photographic production, we understand that photography in the Ottoman Arab world was as much a domestic practice as a foreign import, without necessarily making the latter uncritically mimetic. Early "Arab" photography, like so many other commercial and social practices, unfolded in a mode of seeing the world, a visual regime, that was laid out during the late nineteenth century as *al-nahdah al-'arabiyah* or the "Arab Renaissance." The photography of Palestinian Arab and Armenian photographers worked within the discursive confines of *al-nahdah*. During the nineteenth century, the Ottoman Empire actively engaged in a self-generated juridical, institutional, and social project of "modernity," called Tanzimat, that reached far beyond pedestrian assumptions of "modernization." Rather, an epistemological rupture had occurred where Ottomans themselves were defining an indigenous pathway to modernity. The Arab *nahdah* is an outgrowth of the Ottoman Tanzimat; Arab intellectuals and cultural producers, based in Beirut, Alexandria, and Cairo, but also in Jerusalem, Aleppo and Mosul, were enacting a vision of Arab society and identity that would be comfortable in this "new era," or *al-'asr al-jadid*.[36] The era produced a particular *nahdah* "perspective" (*manzhar*) and *Osmanli* (Ottoman) ideology structured by the priorities and formulae of patriotism, national unity, and "civilization and progress."[37] The visual content, narrative, and priorities of Jawhariyyeh's album roots him and his social milieu squarely within *Osmanli* ideology and the *nahdah* visual regime (fig. 5.4).

Identifying that the *nahdah* and the late Ottoman Empire imbued Jawhariyyeh's worldview is critical to reassessing his use of photography in narrating Palestinian polity and history. The arrangement of the photographs within each album, at times, seems arbitrary, while at others the progression is clearly logical, based on chronology, genre, historic events, personalities, or locality. The relationship between the images and albums does not necessarily correspond to a chronological history, although chronology is the predominant arc. The first five albums are in tighter concert with one another, while the remaining two are almost conceptual in nature. Volume 1 opens with a cavalcade of Ottoman-era portraiture that supplies a diagram of the social networks of Jerusalem and their relationship with Palestinian elites, other provincial capitals, and Istanbul.[38] Volume 1 visualizes the

FIGURE 5.4. Top, from left to right: Sa'adatlu Nasim Bey, Sa'adatlu 'Izzat Bey, Sa'adatlu Rafit Bey 'Atufatlu. Bottom, from left to right: Ibn al-Mutassarif Ru'uf Pasha, 'Atufatlu Ru'uf Pasha, Salid Fa'iq Bey. Jawhariyyeh Album 1, IPS Beirut.

social bedrock of late Ottoman Jerusalem into which Jawhariyyeh was born and that informs Mandate politics.

Volume 2 opens with the arrival of the British (fig. 5.5). It is the album of Palestine's new rulers. It is a new era: World War 1, Arab delegations, Faisal, Abdullah, negotiations, and the breakdown to the riots of Nabi Musa. Volume 3 documents the violent occupation of Palestine, the Revolt of 1929, the rise of Zionist militarism and British oppression, and the internationalization of the Palestine Question. Volume 4 becomes dominated by Zionist settlement, colonial occupation, and violent resistance so that Volume 5, weighed down by the intensity of the preceding two albums, downshifts, opening with large portraits that recenter Palestinian social life around personalities and elites, social hierarchies and social networks. The fifth and the sixth albums rely heavily on Orientalist images, postcards, expatriate, and static images: happy peasants, building projects, processions and religious ceremonies. The final album continues a photographic tour of Jerusalem, building a visual tour from inside the city outward to its surroundings, linking it to Palestine and its geography. This tour of Jerusalem's surroundings

FIGURE 5.5. General and Lady Edmund Allenby. Jawhariyyeh Album 2, IPS Beirut.

may not be as pictorial or romantic as it seems when one remembers that Wasif's father was the Husseini family's representative, responsible for tending to their extensive property holdings surrounding the city. Likewise, Wasif himself worked in the Mandate's Werko office, responsible for land taxation, and we also know that he purchased a large parcel of land in a growing neighborhood of the Palestinian bourgeoisie near Baqa in western Jerusalem.

With the wealth of sources that Jawhariyyeh left us to serve as a foundation of historical inquiry, the question remains: how should we read these albums? This is a methodological question as much as a theoretical one. Did Jawhariyyeh, the Jerusalem musician, arrange his albums like a musical piece, progressing between seven movements, each with their own *maqam?* Perhaps his albums are a visualization of a musical sensibility of history and his experience, arranging a rhythm invisible to some of us but recognizable to a fellow musician? Or, should we read the seven albums as a companion to his two-volume diary to make sense of the cataclysmic events, personalities, social groups, geographies, and institutions depicted in the images? Should we read the albums separate from his written testimony? Should we read the albums with his handwritten index, as he directs us to do in a number of instances within the albums themselves? Or, should we pay attention to the progression of the images, to the unfolding of an illustrated historical narrative that seems to chronologically end in Volume 5 before the end of the albums themselves in Volume 7?

Jawhariyyeh's organization was not a foregone conclusion and the albums were clearly worked over a number of times. Moving between the index and the albums can be confusing as Jawhariyyeh changed his numbering system at least once, leaving us with two cataloguing systems. A handful of images are repeated and events come back to insert themselves in different contexts. We should not take the rhizomic nature of the albums to be an indication of their lack of organization. To the contrary, the conscious over-organization indicates that Jawhariyyeh struggled with the many possible trajectories in which these images could be attached to one another. Therefore, rather than thinking of how to read the images in relation to his written sources—although those sources are crucial—we should attend to the relationship *between* the images within albums and the relationship *between* the albums themselves. While we should not read the images piecemeal per se, at any given instance we can disaggregate each album from the others, reading them singularly. At the same time, we should receive the albums as a unified body where each album leads to the next and each image speaks to those adjacent to it. This method opens the albums to micro and macro readings, where every album and the oeuvre itself functions as a national history. But also, simultaneously, every individual photograph, in any given relation to other photographs, is a lifeworld unto itself in tension with the experiences included and excluded from the albums' visual narrative.

CONTRA NOSTALGIA: TOWARDS MULTIPLE TEMPORALITIES OF PALESTINIAN IDENTITY

Jawhariyyeh's photographs are in sustained tension and dialogue with one another, with history, and with the present. It bears repeating that his albums should not be read nostalgically or through a lens of loss. While Salim Tamari speaks of the melancholy exuded from the albums, particularly not that of Jawhariyyeh himself but, in fact, of his patron. Tamari insists, in fact, that this sense of melancholy should not be confused with nostalgia, as has otherwise been ascribed to Palestinian photography, most notably Walid Khalidi's *Before Their Diaspora*. Khalidi's seminal work introduced a public readership to the Jawhariyyeh collection.[39] Written in 1984, his book offers a tightly organized world of Palestine before 1948. The publication intentionally aims not only to elicit "sympathy" for the Palestinians, who are represented as the oppressed party under Zionist hegemony, but also, consequently, presents a coherent narrative of Palestinian existence before the establishment of the state now known as Israel. This attestation to the presence of Palestinians in historic Palestine directly speaks to colonial practices of pushing colonized people, directly or figuratively, from their own country. Yet the nostalgic air of the narrative partitions a vibrant historical Palestinian society behind the wall of 1948.

Such nostalgia may be understandable and attend to the affective power of photography. For example, Tina Campt offers an invaluable theorization of the "haptic temporalities" of family albums. In examining the intimacy and relationality within the visual archive of the African diaspora, she defines the "haptic encounter" with images of the family album as "multiple forms of touch, which, when understood as constitutive of the sonic frequency of these images, create alternative modalities for understanding the archival temporalities of images." In other words, photographs provide a material space of affective connection to histories, communities, social relations, and even psychic interiorities that the violence of racial capitalism, chattel slavery, colonialist extraction, and settler colonialism work to erase.[40]

While the affective power of the photograph provides corridors to experiences that colonialism seeks to eradicate and invalidate, affect too may be misdirected back to the colonial subject, objectifying the indigenous self as an objectified victim. Lena Meari reminds us how this nostalgic/victimized paradigm structures the international human rights discourse on Palestinians, seeing them as agentless and passive victims of apolitical or depoliticized trauma.[41] Political nostalgia—especially as articulated by those who maintain political and familiar relations with Palestinian ruling families and their familial networks—organizes innumerable written and visual narratives of Palestine and Palestinians. Naseeb Shaheen's two-volume *Pictorial History of Ramallah*, likewise, is a photographic tour de force in itself, a mass of generations of men, women, and children from Ramallah's native families. The publication, he explicitly states, is a "family album" for "the Ramallah people who view the entire town as one extended family."[42] But his photographic narrative is enframed by a very particular temporal conditioning, where the progress of time distances the viewer from a lost Ramallah. It is a photographic scripture for the elders, intentionally written to the "older generation," who will recognize the figures and prominent members of the Ramallah families in ways successive generations will not.[43]

Constance Abdallah's *To Be a Palestinian* reconstructs a memory and history of Palestine through the life of her husband, Hassan Mustafa Hassan Abdallah.[44] Despite its subtitle, *An Anthropology of One Man's Culture*, the book is a personal and rich account of Abdallah's life as a Palestinian, an Arab American, an Arab activist and diplomat. After illustrating the life of Abdallah with images and stories, she casts her husband's as a micro-story and an allegorical history of Betunia, his village. The text mixes personal and family photos with historical, photojournalistic, and postcard images, along with reproductions of art and Palestinian artifacts. In some ways, one might see it as a compendium, or a doppelgänger, to the Jawhariyyeh Collection, or a visual analogue to Salman Abu Sitta's rigorous autobiography *Mapping My Return*. Abu Sitta is known for empirically documenting the erasure of more than four hundred Palestinian villages by the state now known as Israel. His biography's title is not coincidental, offering an autobiographical and factual cartography, his goal to chart "the pieces of debris and painstakingly reconstruct the destroyed landscape," with the explicit intent that "if that could be done," it will be "possible to return to our homes."[45]

Unlike Khalidi's scholarship, Abdallah's biography, and Abu Sitta's cartography for "return" (*al-'awdah*), Jawhariyyeh's photographic narrative, I would argue, does more than document a community before its trauma, "before" al-Nakba, and before the diaspora. Rather, these albums are an animation of a living political, cultural, and social community that *exists* (present tense) as an extension of the photographic albums. The albums' effect is not exclusively an act of documenting, witnessing, testifying, or remembering. Collected over decades and reassembled at least two times after 1948, Jawhariyyeh's albums form a montage, an assembly of disparate narratives to create an album of different speeds and shifts, and a compendium of divergent photographic genres. Whether intentional or not, the archive (and his diaries) speak in, from, and to multiple temporalities or heterochronies. The narrative speaks to Palestine in the present, future, and past tense simultaneously.

To some degree, Raja Shehadeh's *A Rift in Time* suggests how a tension presented by these heterochronies are wired into post-Nakba Palestinian national identity, a tension that inadvertently misdirects us to read Jawhariyyeh's albums as nostalgia. In his book, Shehadeh tours historical Palestine, guided by the figure of his dead uncle Najib Nassar, a character of a past world and a contemporary of Jawhariyyeh.[46] Nassar considered himself an Ottoman citizen and an Arab-Palestinian nationalist. In addition to being the founding editor of, arguably, Palestine's most prominent and important political journal, the anti-Zionist, progressive, and pro-woman al-*Karmil*, Nassar wrote the earliest treatise on Zionism in 1911.[47] Much of this work is a translation of the entry for "Zionism" from the *Jewish Encyclopedia*. However, in this treatise, Nassar is the among the first to correctly identify Zionism as a settler-colonial movement intent on replacing/displacing the indigenous population, Palestinian Arabs, from Palestine. Shehadeh's narrative transports us between multiple historical periods and the present, intertwining Nassar's world with contemporary Palestine where we meet the inhabitants of localities in the Galilee and Golan, among others. On this journey Shehadeh also encounters Palestinians who cannot live in the present but can only live in the past. Abu Naif, for example, can only prattle on about "his glorious years in the 1936 Great Arab Revolt," but "refused to comment on present times."[48] Shehadeh shows that this inability is not a structural part of the Palestinian reality but what one might call a psychological, and perhaps political, defense in order to avoid rather than transcend the hegemony of Zionist occupation.

A Rift in Time is not similar to Jawhariyyeh's work because it is a story of Najib Nassar, a Palestinian subject of the late Ottoman and British Mandate eras. It is similar because it is a story of the physical and social geographies of Palestine and the way those geographies are inhabited by Shehadeh himself in multiple temporalities. That Palestine is inaccessible, occupied, and more than four hundred villages lie in rubble does not preclude the reality that Palestine is unified in a historical present. Shahadeh's literary tour of historic Palestine commutes between the historical and the present. He co-inhabits the world of his "Ottoman uncle," Najib Nassar, and his own contemporary self. In Jawhariyyeh's photographic archive, Palestine lives at the juncture of two synchronized temporalities contained in one empirical reality: Palestine and Palestinian society exist in an unbroken continuity from the Ottoman period to the current day. Jawhariyyeh collected photographs over his lifetime, speaking to a future that was imminent. His visual narration of Palestine is not exclusively a historical documentary. Like *A Rift in Time*, his albums are a *documentary of the present*, a visualization that exists even in exile and under occupation. If Palestinians have been displaced and their homes wiped out, their history has not and the present is constantly in the process of being reclaimed.

Musée Imaginaire Palestinien

The photography albums arise out of the "Jawhariyyeh Collection," a collection of Palestinian and Arab art, textiles, instruments, furniture, and photographs that Jawhariyyeh collected throughout his lifetime. Traveling from his Jerusalem home to the West Bank and eventually Beirut, the collection itself has its own story that remains at the margins of his written narrative and is absent from his photography albums altogether.

His narrative, his albums, and indeed the Jawhariyyeh Collection share two elementary yet essential qualities. The first is that each was intended to be seen and read, first and foremost, by Palestinians and Arabs. Secondly, his oeuvre is a marked by a glaring self-awareness. Individually and collectively, his writing and albums are a conscious project, part nationalist (Palestinian), part communal (Jerusalemite, Orthodox, and Jawhariyyeh family-network), part personal, and, as we have seen, part historical and part contemporary. This self-awareness coupled with a clear intentionality that the photographs were to be viewed by Palestinians spurs us to theorize about the use of photography in producing (or reproducing) a historical narrative of Palestine. The lack of intimacy, even salaciousness, of the photography mirror its intent. In this regard, we may understand Jawhariyyeh's *Tarikh Falastin al-musawwar* less as an illustrated history than as Palestine's first national museum.[49]

The museum is an institution where nation-states and their enfranchised citizens instrumentalize their power and propagate dominant discourses. The museum is where states and their constituent actors visualize and condense national normativity and naturalize a victorious national selfhood and its relation to the state itself, its environs, and the natural world. The museum offers states and their citizens an opportunity to imagine and materialize their *weltanschauung* and their place in it. Jawhariyyeh's photograph albums are an answer to a museum for a stateless people.

In his diary, Jawhariyyeh specifically states that the Jawhariyyeh Collection was intended to be a "kind of national museum under the slogan: *This is our legacy that speaks of who we are, so behold it when we are gone.*"[50] The Collection figures prominently in his diary, where he specifically calls the room of his house where it is held "the Museum." Jawhariyyeh pays particular reverence to British military governor Ronald Storr (fig. 5.6), who was an avid antiquarian and aficionado of Middle Eastern artifacts, and who inspired Jawhariyyeh to begin collecting. He remarks that Storr's home in Mulk al-Alman (the German Colony) was like a museum. In seeing it, he states, the Governor's home made him "realize the dream I had always nourished inside to start acquiring memorabilia and antiques, which led to my hopes turning into reality."[51]

Jawhariyyeh describes the Collection almost in the language of magical realism. He notes how the photographs of singers, composers, and musicians enraptured his guest the Jewish-Egyptian singer Khairiyah al-Saqqa.[52] When British soldiers break into his house searching for weapons in the wake of the 1929 uprising, the collection bedazzles them, distracting them until they leave without searching the premises.[53] Even the house itself has an enchanted quality. His marital home in Nicophoria, a neighborhood of Jerusalem, was the ideal setting for Palestinian artifacts, displayed in an "old Arab-style building with cross-vault arches." The dilapidated structure was transformed by Jawhariyyeh and his bride from a house into a "spectacular museum."[54] It housed china from his father, snakeskins,

FIGURE 5.6. Ronald Storrs, British Mandate Governor of Jerusalem, in front of the entrance to the British Opthalmic Hospital on the Jerusalem-Bethlehem road, being received by a contingent of Jerusalem police. Jawhariyyeh Album 2, IPS Beirut.

a "Cairo-made armchair inlaid with mother of pearl," a "long Ibrahim Pasha flint lock rifle," and a Persian belt used as a curtain. The walls were adorned "with historical pictures and portraits of loved ones such as my late father, the late Hussein Effendi al-Husseini, and others, in oriental Damascene frames, which added to the room's elegance and beauty."[55]

In 1948, Jawhariyyeh's collection ceased to be a bricks-and-mortar museum, planted in a particular neighborhood within Jerusalem and within a particular home, where its objects quite explicitly and intentionally were placed in concert with other objects. Here, photography's fundamental qualities of mobility and reproducibility, the "itinerant" nature of photography, assert themselves most forcefully, defying the project of historical, physical, and discursive erasure that colonial-settler powers intend over conquered and colonized lands. For Jawhariyyeh the photography archive was not an archive of ambivalence but an archive of certainty. It speaks across and through time to Palestinians in a prescient way: *behold it when we are gone.* The photographs' indexical statements were factual attestations to social realities that could not be appropriated as easily as people's homes and lands. Photography albums are the disembodied soul of a hardscaped living museum, but also of the social networks embedded in those objects. The photographs become the raw material for the *musée imaginaire*, the museum without walls, of Palestine.

Yet, the *musée imaginaire palestinien* is, perhaps, a precedent for and an inversion of André Malraux's *musée imaginaire*.[56] Malraux was concerned with objects of art. He was searching for the purity of their art-ness as objects. In all the "imagination" of his museum, Malraux, steeped in the modern tradition of art as aesthetic-contemplative object, intuitively understood objects as plundered and looted objects. Museums, he wrote, "imposed on the spectator a wholly new attitude toward the work of art. For they have tended to estrange the works they bring together from their original functions. . . ."[57] Art was originally tied to a context, a setting, time, period, its social relations and a dominant aesthetic regime. For Malraux, the violence of the museum is its edificial characteristic, the arbitrary mixing of objects brought together through institutional (and state) power. His *musée imaginaire*, or "museum without walls" would free objects from the over-determination of their contexts and liberate their potentiality as art objects, allowing them to occupy a shared aesthetic realm. Within this context, the invention of photography revolutionized our relationship to art, allowing us to close the proximity between masterpieces and the viewers, between spaces of spectatorship and the objects of art. Photography redefined the notion of masterpieces and allowed other styles and genres to enter into the realm of art (further divorcing the objects from their social contexts and geographic limitations).

Unlike Malraux, Jawhariyyeh was a man of the state, both the Ottoman state and the Mandate government. For all of his talent as a musician, in the end, he was a *petit-fonctionnaire*, closely associated with and genuinely loyal to Jerusalem's ruling elites. If we were to romanticize Jawhariyyeh and his albums as the revolutionary project of a libertine musician, we would not only exaggerate Wasif's true ability to negotiate and uphold the ruling order, which he served. We would, more importantly, be distracted from the regime of visuality which he reproduced and how it was intimately entwined with "Arab modernity," capital, and local and imperial power (whether British or Ottoman).

This present analysis is not concerned with Malraux's larger theory or psychology of art and art history. It is not concerned with how he expands the value of the aesthetics of the art object, although aesthetics' relationship to "visuality" is certainly relevant to understanding the Jawhariyyeh albums. I am not even taking an interest in how Malraux expands the aesthetic value of deracinated non-Western objects, placing them on the same plane as Western "masterpieces" (no doubt, a cultural appreciation he developed during his years in China and Vietnam). Malraux here only is an opportunity to open the possibilities for a "potential history" of plundered objects, (and objects that will be plundered). This potential history of these photographs does not intend to "reveal that these objects were looted, since this is not secret," as Azoulay teaches us.[58] Rather, we invert insights from Malraux's Eurocentric imagination to delink objects through the medium of photography within the context of the colonized, "in order to enable the rights in these looted objects to be recognized" as objects belonging to "a built world" beyond the epistemology of a colonial moment that can only metabolize them through Orientalist (on the one hand) and nationalist (on the other) social relations.[59]

Otherwise said, what should interest us is Malraux's observation that the medium of photography changes the nature of social relations between object and viewers and between objects themselves. A photograph can put art objects from disparate origins and temporalities within a radically new proximity, a proximity that otherwise would be impossible, thereby creating new relationships between them. For Jawhariyyeh photographs, when conjoined to the physical space of his home and locality, form a part of his larger collection, acting in dialogue with the other objects in his "museum," including instruments, "traditional" furniture, textiles and ceramics, and images of prominent figures. 1948 did not change the

FIGURE 5.7. Receiving the flag of the Prophet Musa from Dar al-Raghib and an Egyptian music troup, 1919. Jawhariyyeh Album 2, IPS Beirut.

nature of Palestinian photographs, despite wrenching them away from their collector, their space, and the objects around them. Rather, 1948 changed their responsibilities. The responsibilities of the albums after 1948 transformed the photographs themselves into testimonial artifacts, legal and historical documents, and supplements for the objects that were stolen. 1948 demanded that Jawhariyyeh convert material objects into witnesses of history, not vice-versa.

When we speak of an imaginary, then, I certainly do not mean fantasies, but rather reach to the play of imagination as image-nation, of Jawhariyyeh imaging/imagining a nation by deploying material Palestinian objects, figures, events, and references. But imagination also alludes to the Palestinian *imago*, in the psychoanalytic sense. Jawhariyyeh's imagination of Palestine and Palestinian social relations assembles images as documents of empirical-indexical reality and narrates a Palestine of the present that is imbricated with the past.

This is not a theoretical imposition on the work. In his diaries, Jawhariyyeh repeatedly invites his readers to "imagine." He says, "Imagine an evening like that, in a cafe, after a day at work!"[60] In describing the frenetic excitement in Jerusalem's streets during Holy Week which he amply represents in his albums (fig. 5.7), where Muslims simultaneous celebrated the Feast of Moses while mixing with Palestinian Christians and foreigners in Jerusalem, he exclaims, "Imagine what Jerusalem was like on this Holy Thursday, as Christians from the various denominations held an unequaled celebration in which they were joined by foreign tourists and pilgrims visiting the Holy City. Then imagine the gathering of Muslims who were either from the city itself or from neighboring villages."[61] Likewise, in juxtaposing the sensory experiences of enjoying an overflowing spring in the village of Silwan after a month of rain causing sewage to wash down from Jerusalem, he states, "so imagine us picnicking and washing our feet in the pure water of Bir Ayyub, while before us, alas, flowed a large river of foul-smelling waste."[62] In his diary and photographic albums, imagination is not abstract or fantastic. It is empirical. It is a "redistribution of the sensible."[63]

Jawhariyyeh's *musée imaginaire palestinien* is mediated by images often produced not by Palestinians, by the people who inhabited and claimed propriety of those spaces and places, but by those whose Holy Land and colonialist narratives diminished their very presence and negated the legitimacy of their claims to those spaces and places. It is not surprising, then, that he opens his albums with a constellation of *cartes de visite* and cabinet cards testifying to the social contracts and relations between families, individuals, institutions, and classes within Jerusalem and Palestine. While not central to these relationships, Jawhariyyeh is the linchpin, connecting for us a complex set of social, political, economic, and communal relations that span three generations and quite a bit of geography. The photographs, including portraits and their dedications, trace the social vectors and subjective ideals that were so central to Jawhariyyeh's personal and professional *weltanschauung*, an ideological world richly described in his autobiographical writing.

DEEP SPACE OF PALESTINIAN PHOTOGRAPHY: PALESTINE AS A SOCIAL FACT

The portrait gallery in Jawhariyyeh's first album is an invitation to the viewer, or spectator, to enter the ambulatory of a *musée imaginaire*. This ambulatory creates a space for witnessing the bedrock of political and social networks that link people and communities to localities. Didi-Huberman warns us that ignoring "the dialectic work of images" puts us at risk of "confusing fact with fetish, archive with appearance, work with manipulation." It, then, seems obvious to think of Jawhariyyeh's photographic collection as something more than a mimetic reproduction of Storr's collecting practice. Nor should we see it as a canned curatorial impulse, spurred by nationalism, fetishization, or nostalgia. Rather, to purloin from Didi-Huberman, the images of Jawhariyyeh's museum without walls are deployed "according to the minimum complexity supposed by two points that confront each other under the gaze of a third."[64] The photographs supplement a space of cultural identification and political assertion that is otherwise physically inaccessible due to Zionist larceny. But also, photographs put in motion the play of Palestinian objects, events, actors, and localities with the gaze of the Palestinian subject of the present. It is this parallax, this triangulated vision, that organizes Jawhariyyeh's albums, which otherwise may seem staccato, capricious, and disjointed.

FIGURE 5.8. Left: Hussein Hashim Effendi al-Husseini; right: Faidi Effendi al-ʿAlami. Jawhari-yyeh Album 1, IPS Beirut.

Any given image in Jawhariyyeh's albums is an invitation to the Palestinian spectator to enter the *musée imaginaire*, and locate oneself in history and the present through a visual triangulation. This parallax vision organizes the images of Jawhariyyeh's albums, where every image is connected to several other photographs in a myriad of ways representing not only what I have called elsewhere a dense "network of sociability" inherent to pre-1948 Palestinian social and political life, but also the deep social space of Palestinian social relations that cuts across time and legitimate a lasting claim to historic Palestine.[65] Let us explore this dense web and deep space of the photograph through a few rudimentary examples.

Portraits of Faidi al-ʿAlami and Hussein al-Husseini (fig. 5.8) are among the local elites in the first pages of Volume 1. Likely taken by the Krikorian studio, these are more than tributary portraits of prominent Palestinians. Rather, these images connect and are in conversation with a number of other images in subsequent volumes. Faidi al-ʿAlami was a Palestinian Ottoman official and Ottoman Parliamentarian. He was mayor (1906–09) when Jerusalem's clock tower at Bab al-Khalil was completed. Wasif gives us a detailed history of the clock, which is the most frequently represented photograph in his albums (fig. 5.9). The clock, we are

FIGURE 5.9. *Bab al-Khalil as I knew it during the Ottoman Era, 1910.* Jawhariyyeh Album 5, IPS Beirut.

told, was constructed to commemorate the twenty-five-year celebration of Sultan Abdülhamid's rule. Seven clock towers were constructed in the Palestinian cities of Jaffa, al-Nasirah (Nazareth), Nablus, Haifa, Safad, and 'Akka. The architect was Pascal Effendi Serufim, the municipality's architect and a member of "one of the most honorable families of the Roman Catholic community of Jerusalem."[66] Pascal apparently also was active with a small handful of indigenous, European Christian, and European Jewish architects in designing and building new quarters in Jerusalem in the early part of the century for Jewish settlers.[67] He was hired in 1902 by the Italian consulate to "restore the house bought on behalf of the Empress Taytu [of Ethiopia]."[68] Jawhariyyeh likens him to the musician Muhammad Abdul-Wahhab because he studied in France but "adhered to the Oriental architectural style," practicing the "Franco-Arab" architecture. The clock had an "important role in Jerusalem and was of great use to its citizens," and it "could be even seen from as far away as Beit Laham (Bethlehem)."[69] Yet, "despite its perfect construction, the quality of its stones, and its ornamentation," Ronald Storrs's Pro Jerusalem Society "demolished it overnight," considering it was out of place with the Wall's "four hundred years of history" (fig. 5.10).[70]

While Jawhariyyeh agreed with Storrs, he proposes that it could have been moved to the rooftop of the Barclays building or the new municipality building (fig. 5.11). Lamenting the loss of the town, he discloses that he made a wooden model of the clock tower and Bab al-Khalil: "thus I have immortalized the entrance to the

FIGURE 5.10. Ronald Storrs. Jawhariyyeh Album 2, IPS Beirut.

FIGURE 5.11. Barclays Bank. Jawhariyyeh Album 5, IPS Beirut.

city as it was on the eve of the British occupation."[71] The model was a part of the Jawharriyah Collection but, Tamari and Nassar tell us, it was gone when Wasif's acquaintance returned to retrieve it in 1967 with other objects from his collection. There may be another reason for the ample number of images of the Bab al-Khalil clock tower, other than the important fact that Hamidian clocktowers marked the

FIGURE 5.12. Professors at the National School. Sitting, right to left: Adel Jabar, Achille Saikali, Khalil Sakakini, Antoni Mashabak, Musa al-ʿAlami, Hanna Hamadah, George Khamis. Jawhariyyeh Album 2, IPS Beirut.

political and economic importance of Arab provincial cities. The Vesters, who ran the American Colony and sold postcards produced by their Photography Department, had a thriving tourist shop at Jaffa Gate.

These social relations not only structure the past but also structure and reach into Jawhariyyeh's present. Al-ʿAlami's father was Musa al-ʿAlami, a former Mayor of Jerusalem. His son was also Musa, named after his grandfather. Musa, the junior, was an eminent Arab nationalist who had studied law at Cambridge. He appears in a portrait of the faculty of the National School, with other renowned educators and nationalists (fig. 5.12). He returned to Palestine to work with the British Mandate government, until he was exiled by the British for advocacy of Palestinian liberation. His sister, Niʾmati, married Jamal Husseini, another prominent Arab nationalist activist who was also sent into exile and participated in the anti-Zionist movement and anti-British struggle. They all (save Niʾmati) are represented in a number of different individual and group portraits throughout the albums.

Faidi al-ʿAlami was preceded as mayor by Hussein Hashim al-Husseini (also known as Hussein Salim al-Husseini), who held office during the CUP Revolution. Hussein was the son of Salim, notable late nineteenth-century mayor of Jerusalem and brother of Musa Kazhim al-Husseini. Musa Kazhim regularly appears in Jawhariyyeh's albums, as does Hussein al-Husseini. Musa Kazhim was a high-level Ottoman official, prominent Palestinian nationalist, and head of the Executive Committee of the Palestine Arab Congress. Musa Kazhim was also the uncle of Jamal al-Husseini, Musa al-ʿAlami's son-in-law. Visually, Hussein

FIGURE 5.13. Martyr 'Ali bin Hussain Hashim al-Husseini. Jawhariyyeh Album 3, IPS Beirut.

Salim al-Husseini is best known as the mayor of Jerusalem who surrendered the city to the British during World War 1, an image we have seen earlier in this book. Hussein's son, 'Ali (fig. 5.13), who appears in the albums, was martyred after he joined the armed resistance against British rule during the Great Revolt. In 1938, he was killed in battle at Bani Na'im against the British, under the command of the

FIGURE 5.14. Martyr 'Ali bin Hussain Hashim al-Husseini with cousin and hero 'Abd al-Qadir al-Hussein. Jawhariyyeh Album 3, IPS Beirut.

legendary 'Abd al-Qadir al-Husseini, son of Musa Kazhim al-Husseini (fig. 5.14). 'Ali and the famous 'Abd al-Qadir were cousins.

Hussein al-Husseini also, as we have seen, had a special relationship with Wasif, effectively adopting him after his father's death in 1914. In his diary, Jawhariyyeh tells us much about Hussein, including a large section about his paramour,

Persifon, who was a successful merchant and respected citizen of the city. One of his crowning achievements in Jawhariyyeh's opinion was to bring the musician Sheikh Salama Hijazi and George Abyad's performance troupes from Cairo. An enormous tent was erected for the performance, and the plays *Salah al-din* (probably written by Farah Antun) and *Romeo and Juliet* were performed to great acclaim. Hijazi's performance was so moving, Jawhariyyeh states, that it drove Greeks to tears. The young Jawhariyyeh attended the performance with his father, who was employed in Elias Effendi Habib's office at the time.

Jawhariyyeh could not have foreseen how his "hopes" and "dream" of collecting objects and chronicling the lives, social networks and events of Jerusalem would create an imaginary palimpsest where every image triangulates between individuals, events, and places of the past and the Palestinian spectator of the present. The portrait gallery of his photographic *musée imaginaire* announces that the seven albums are, in fact, the first Palestinian national museum without walls, one that is based not in cultural artifacts and art objects but in a multi-dimensional social network. Unlike Malraux's concept, Jawhariyyeh's *musée imaginaire* did not recode the relationship between art objects, divorcing them from their historical contexts and social relations in order to produce new aesthetic meaning for those objects. To the contrary, the photography albums represent the deep space of a trans-temporal social and political reality; they produce a space to attest and testify to the historical contexts and social relations of the photographic objects and sitters that are denied by Zionist expropriation.

The *musée imaginaire palestinien*, however, is more than just a series of legal documents salvaged from the wreck of al-Nakba. It is more than artifacts for reconstructing social relations that functioned at the heart of a society whose existence is denied by many Israelis, or US Presidents and Congressmen and Congresswomen. It is more than stubborn shards of history that will not go away. The photography albums of Jawhariyyeh "redistribute the sensible" in order to bring together deceased, living, and future individuals in a single space and back into their natural order, revealing how these individuals congregate with one another in a sensibility that defies *partage* and flouts the violence thrust upon them, individually, and their community, collectively, by settler-colonialism. As a consequence of this redistribution of the sensible, Jawhariyyeh's *musée imaginaire palestinien* produces and reproduces social relations and social meaning, offering not an "alternate" history but a social reality that stands in defiance of a Zionist alternative history qua History.

Rancière asserts that the distribution of the sensible reveals who "can have a share in what is common to the community based on what they do and on the time and space in which this activity is performed."[72] It is a matter of how images, and indeed aesthetics, are collectively shared, embodied, experienced, felt, perceived, created, owned, and/or disavowed in ways that stand outside but are also engaged with formal means and regimes of sovereignty and governance. He continues,

"Having a particular 'occupation' thereby determines the ability or inability to take charge of what is common to the community: it defines what is visible or not in a common space, endowed with a common language, etc."[73] Rancière means "occupation" as work or labor. Yet, the elision of "occupation" (as a parapraxis within the context of Palestine) transfers and discloses how Rancière's critique can be made more relevant to the context of settler-colonialism. The distribution of the sensible is determined by *occupation* and/or refusal of it. Jawhariyyeh's *musée imaginaire palestinien* realigns the sensible and the sensibility of photographs under occupation. The boundaries of this partition are not mediated by Zionist domination but rather, mediated by a regime of photographic visuality that understands the Palestinians as social facts to Palestine, regardless of international *partage* and in defiance of occupation.

THE NACHLEBEN ALBUMS

Jawhariyyeh's albums are circumscribed by two parallel temporalities—a temporality of the late Ottoman and Mandate eras and a temporality of post-1948—bound by a singular regime of visuality. The albums should not be seen, as Khalidi's work proposes, as partitioned pre-and post 1948, but as a redistributing of the sensible, repartitioning a regime of visuality that binds the two temporalities together through the position of the Palestinian spectator. The simultaneity of two coterminous temporalities is the state of all Palestinian photographs before 1948. It has been a mistake to see photographs as artifacts of the past and as documents of history alone. Rather, they survive as material objects that bind the past and present as they bind the present and future. In this regard, Jawhariyyeh's albums are an assemblage, a concert, of perpetual "surviving images."

A surviving image, in Didi-Huberman's words, "is an image that, having lost its original use, value and meaning, nonetheless comes back, like a ghost, at a particular historical moment: a moment of 'crisis,' a moment when it demonstrates latency, its tenacity, its vivacity, and its 'anthropological adhesion.'"[74] The English term "survival" was frequently used interchangeably with *nachleben*, "the mysterious keyword or slogan of [Aby] Warburg's entire enterprise, *Nachleben de Antike*," in order to make us consider the "afterlife" of art object and images.[75] Simply put, "nachleben meant making historical time more complex, recognizing specific, non-natural temporalities in the cultural world. . . ."[76]

Within the context of Palestine, "survival" becomes something more powerful, current, and salient, something certainly rooted in Aby Warburg's use of *nachleben* but also something that is grossly absent from Didi-Huberman's work in general. That is, *nachleben* as an analytic concept arises from what Didi-Huberman (partially quoting Warburg) called the "displaced" terrain of [Warburg's] travels in Hopi country."[77] Warburg, perhaps better than Didi-Huberman, understood intuitively the politics and presence of indigenous people living in a settler-colonial society under the constant pressure of erasure. Indigeneity under settler-colonial violence is imminent to Warburg's concept of *nachleben*, a concept that brings "displaced" temporalities and lived-worlds into the realm of perception. Jawhariyyeh's repurposed images are not ghostly figures of the past, but they are haunted by the present and future. In fact, they are a refusal to become a specter of the past, a refusal to go away. They are, like the indigenous Hopi objects and images in Warburg's archive, an insistence of reality. If the presence of the Palestinians is latent, they, like the Hopi, are only latent in the mind and tradition of the colonizer. But to the indigenous spectator, the Palestinian, they are imbricated in the temporality of an unbroken past-present-future continuum of social reality: Palestine.

It is not lost on us that Warburg's nachleben emerges from this engagement with the first nations of what is now known as North America. These links between settler colonialism in the country now known as the United States and in Palestine has been noted by a number of scholars, from Steven Salaita to J. Kēhaulani Kauanui.[78] Like the Palestinian photographic archive, Hopi cultural objects did not present new possibilities to recover a lost history for the Hopi people. Rather, unbeknownst to Warburg, they really were an invitation *to see history as it is*, outside the *"displaced terrain"* of Euro-American history as History. If this analysis is an overwriting of Warburg's Taylorian ethnography of Hopi "art," it is productive because it allows us to understand exactly what is going on in Jawhariyyeh's photography albums. That is, the albums are not a rectification of history, a reintroduction of Palestinian history into History, or a reintroduction into the field of photographic visuality. Rather, they are a narrativization of history through a dominant Arab visuality that European and Zionist histories have tried to unsuccessfully imagine out of History, to displace out of the visual geographies that started with Orientalism and continue to today.

When we read Jawhariyyeh's albums as one continuous text over several volumes, we might be "disoriented," searching for a clean narrative of "before the diaspora." Monumental portraits shift to war images, images of riots and corpses, to Palestinian, Arab, and Muslim delegations contrasting British diplomatic images; the photojournalism of current affairs is juxtaposed against a closing litany of Orientalist and colonial postcards. Yet, what occurs with the adjacency of a myriad of images is a metabolizing of the images into a history that "disorients" the colonizer's History. The images next to images disorient not only through introducing a mélange of coterminous heterochronies, but they liberate subaltern and unrepresented experiences, freeing them to burst forth from below the dominant regime of visuality that constituted Arab modernity in Palestine.

This disorienting history is a dissensual history. It is a history of contradictory multitudes that holds temporalities in a counter-hegemonic visuality (counter-hegemonic to colonial visuality). Such a statement in any other context might be seen as a cliché. But in a Palestine governed by the logic of settler colonialism, the idea of a "conflictual" history is not permitted. Such claims make Palestinians immediately vulnerable to dispossessing relativism, to a history presupposed upon a series of rival opinions, equal but rival claims, or "alternative" but equally valid perspectives. In the case of Palestine, I am arguing for a dissensual history that does prioritize material dispossession over fantastic historical claims to ownership.

Dissensual history, rather, is something more, I am arguing. It involves an acknowledgment of the contradictions with Arab capitalist modernity but also an acknowledgment of a history of the will to liberation and the desire to self-determination, of the Arab people and, especially, of the Palestinian people. Dissensual history is a "demonstration (*manifestation*) of a gap in the sensible itself," in Rancière's words.[79] The photographic album is a *demonstration*, a *manifestation* in French and *muzhahirah* in Arabic, of the political in a way that Didi-Huberman cannot fathom. That is, it is "a demonstration that makes visible that which has no reason to be seen; it places one world in another."[80] Hence, the images are not haunted, but a haunting. Even more accurately, Jawhariyyeh's photographs are a form of seizure, a re-appropriation, a refusal of partition.

The Orientalist and colonialist photographic archive houses and organizes an imminent desire to expel Arabs (like all colonized peoples) out of their own history and out of their own visual geographies. Zionism is only the enactment of that colonial, Orientalist fantasy. Yet Jawhariyyeh's albums are precisely about the facticity of the Palestinian spectators, who asserts their presence in the photograph, in the land, and in Palestine, regardless of who produced those images. They claim these photographs as visual articulations of Palestinian national legitimacy and national rights as well as subjective presence. They claim the *kawshun* (title) over the index and over Palestine, historically and in the present. This claim, again, is not one of the sanctity of private property or the "rights" to property or the sanctity of the rights of individuals. The albums are a collective authorization and licensing of the title as testimony (*shahadah*) to their place in their communal space, in their home, in their history and in their present. The albums are a *manifestation*, a demonstration, of the refusal to be pushed out of a history not fully of their making.

This analysis should not be seen as conceptual. It is meant be understood quite literally. Images of protest and demonstrations figure prominently in Wasif's albums. It is important to note that photographs of the Nabi Musa "riots" of 1920, the 1921 Jaffa riots, the 1929 Buraq uprising, and the 1933 demonstrations conspicuously emerge as images that one cannot help but to consider as the retroactively projected violence of 1948. The photographs of protests and violence show the burned and ransacked homes of Jews, probably from the Old Yishuv in Jerusalem and al-Khalil (Hebron), as readily as Palestinian corpses (fig. 5.15). More specifically, after the provocations of Rightist Zionists at the Wailing Wall, violence broke out in 1929, resulting in the death of 116 Palestinians and 133 Jews in what is known as the Buraq Revolt, which, in the words of historical Rana Barakat, grew to become "a collective and cohesive expression of resistance to British colonial

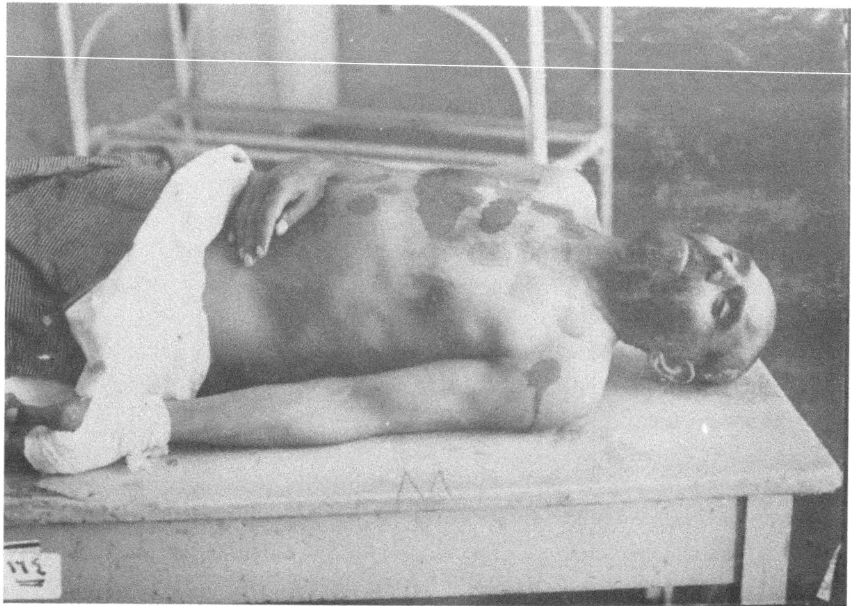

FIGURE 5.15. Ahmad ʿAwwad al-Liftawi, killed by Zionists during the Buraq Revolt, September 1, 1929. Jawhariyyeh Album 2, IPS Beirut.

rule and its implicit endorsement of Zionist settler colonialism."[81] Alongside Palestinian attacks on the Old Yishuv and settlers from the New Yishuv, and as a consequence of peasant organizing, Palestinian political society launched a series of nonviolent protests. As this is the class that Wasif served and was connected to, he represents demonstrations and conferences organized by the Palestinian ruling class at *Rawdat al-Maʾarif* (fig. 5.16).

Images of congresses, demonstrations, strikes, and protests throughout Palestine are well represented, and show us that along with the usual notable and middle class (male) Palestinians, peasants, Bedouin, and working-class people attended in significant numbers. Group portraits of congresses, conferences, and meetings among a variety of Palestinians appear often and, like the two images of the Khalidi Library, images of conferences such as a group of "Male Arab Politicians" are reproduced at different angles, as seen in almost the exact same group portrait in the introduction of this book. Among these sets of images, two sets of protest photos, however, stick out. The first is a series of photographs of the Arab Women's Executive Committee engaged in a public action. The images are also found in the Matson Collection, now housed in the Library of Congress, suggesting that the photographs were taken by the American Colony. Julie Peteet and Ellen Fleischmann, respectively, mark the growth and activism of a robust anti-colonialist and anti-Zionist Arab women's movement in Palestine since the end

FIGURE 5.16. *Arab politicians at Rawdat al-Ma'arif, 1929. First row: Raghib Nashishibi, Musa Kazhim al-Husseini, al-Hajj Amin al-Husseini, 'Awni 'Abd al-Hadi. Second row: Sulaiman Tuqan . . . Hussain 'Aziz (Egyptian Consul in Jerusalem), al-Hajj Toufiq Hamad, Amin al-Tamimi, al-Hajj Sa'id al-Shawwa. Third row: . . . .Yusuf 'Ashur (father of Issam 'Ashur) . . . .Mustafa al-Khalidi near the aisle, 'Adil Jabar on the left of the aisle, and Ahmad 'al-Akki.* Photo: Khalik Sakakini. Jawhariyyeh Album 3, IPS Beirut.

of World War 1, including forming a delegation to meet the British High Commission in 1920 to insist on the abrogation of the Balfour Declaration.[82] Since that time, Peteet notes, women from a cross-section of Palestinian society have regularly appeared in street demonstrations, many of which turned violent (largely at the instigation of the British or Zionists). The Committee was the Executive of the Arab Women's Association, launched at the Palestine Arab Women's Congress in 1929 as a direct result of the Buraq uprising. It was attended by a cross-section of women from the new middle ("effendi") classes, the upper class, and those from notable families from throughout Palestine.[83]

The Arab Women's Executive Committee engaged in civil acts of protest, hoping to deliver their memorandum to the High Commissioner's wife, who refused to meet them. As a result, they "had no other alternative but to wait upon the High Commissioner at the Government House, and to ignore all traditional restrictions."[84] Fleischmann's careful history of the formation of the Arab Women's Association (AWA) challenges the foundational narrative that the Executive Committee was founded upon the return from the AWA's first congress after women's delegations presented a resolution to the British High Commissioner and visited

FIGURE 5.17. Arab Women's Executive Committee Protest, British High Command, 1929. Jawhariyyeh Album 2, IPS Beirut.

a number of foreign consuls. Rather than mapping discrepancies in "divergent" historical accounts, Fleischmann notes that the "confusion" between them accents the "political sophistication of the congress organizers, who recognized the importance of public perceptions of their political behavior."[85] This sophistication, organization, and commitment comes through in the Jawhariyyeh albums.

The series of images depict the women's delegation congregating outside an archway, wall, staircase, and in a cavalcade of cars (fig. 5.17). The women are at ease and, in some images, laughing. Some women are covered and others are not. They all look determined and comfortable in their space, waiting to make their intervention. The American Colony's Photography Service likely is responsible for these images as well as the iconic image of the meeting at Rawdat al-Maʿarif. The American Colony's Matson Collection at the Library of Congress has a similar image of the women delegates waiting outside the house of the High Commissioner, John Chancellor. Jawhariyyeh, however, presents four images on one page. Two photographs show women outside the house of ʿAwni ʿAbd al-Hadi. Cofounder of the Istiqlal Party and, later, a member of the Arab Higher Committee, he also appears in the images of the Arab Congress at Rawdat al-Ma'arif. His wife, Tarab 'Abd al-Hadi, was a leading member of the feminist nationalist movement and, therefore, it is likely that the delegates congregated at her house. From there, they organized a caravan of automobiles, as shown in another photograph, to Chancellor's residence. Jawhariyyeh places the four images in relation to images of their male counterparts' demonstrations, signaling the coordinated and comprehensive organizing underway in Palestinian political and civil society. But he also places the images in relation to one another, four images of the same day in a dynamic unfolding. Placed in relation to one another, they provide a visual narrative that animates the work of these activists in a way that is otherwise not communicated through a singular, static image in the American Colony collection.

These images reveal a dissensual history. Certainly, one readily reaches to the issue of women's participation in the nationalist movement. The activism of women is often displaced or forgotten. Or worse, it is claimed as an uncritical tokenism that offers no critique of gender and class disparities within Palestinian Arab society at that time. In other words, we can also see the way in which class privilege within nationalist organizing displaces the *gendered* nature of these women's critiques, asking us to read them as "patriots," not as critics of the male ruling power to which many were intimately attached.[86] The images point to a class and political struggle within the Palestinian ruling classes and within Palestinian society writ large. Yet, as we have seen in chapter 3, the Jawhariyyeh photography albums present the male-dominated surface of Arab social history. This all-male surface, however, is saturated with and fully structured by the lives, labor, and relationships of women. With this in mind, we must approach the appearance of any women, even ruling elite women, as a breach of a veneer of their absence that speaks to their sheer centrality of women's role of social reproduction, as Tithi Bhattacharya, Nancy Fraser, Cinzia Arruzza, and Silvia Federici teach us.[87]

The Arab Women's Executive Committee's members were from the economic and political elite and perhaps their representation should point us to the absence of working and peasant class women in Palestinian society in Jawhariyyeh's albums. Yet, the archeology of this photographic archive does provide us with a breach of that masculinist gendered surface. Like Tarab 'Abd al-Hadi, a number of these women had husbands on the Arab Executive Committee and its successor, the Arab Higher Committee.[88] These were the elites who had structured Palestinian society since the late Ottoman era and who populated Jawhariyyeh's social life and albums. Approaching the images from an oblique, gendered dissensual angle, images of "demonstrations" allow gender (and class) tension to seep from Jawhariyyeh's male and ruling-class centered narrative. On the one hand, these images inadvertently document the disintegration, ineffectual nature, and collusion, of the ruling families and their functionaries and clients, including Jawhariyyeh himself. But, perhaps on the other, these images remind us of the central of women in the reproduction of a people, their social ties and their cultural identities that defy erasure, whether by Arab masculinist narratives or by Zionist settler colonialism.

Let us read the gendered images of the Arab Women's Executive Committee against equally frenetic images that were put in motion with one another by Jawhariyyeh. While the riots of Nabi Musa and the conflagration of 1929 regularly receive attention and figure prominently in the written and visual narrative of the history of Palestine, the "Jaffa Protest" of 1933 receives less attention. By 1933, Jewish immigration began to further intensify due to worsening conditions for Jews in Nazi Germany. Furthermore, Palestine's new High Commissioner, Arthur Wauchope, was a consummate colonial-military governor. He was also an unabashed and open Zionist sympathizer, committed to Jewish economic and political development in Palestine, including support for the militarization of the Yishuv. After discovering a shipment of arms headed to Tel Aviv, the Arab Executive Committee called for a general strike in October of 1933, sparking a series of demonstrations throughout Palestine, starting in Jerusalem and spreading to Jaffa, Haifa, and Nablus. Tali Hatuka notes that the events of 1933 clearly differed from the uprisings in 1920, 1921 and 1929, which were directed at Zionists and Arab Jews.[89] These demonstrations protested specifically against what had become clear as the British Mandate's open support for the Zionist project and were a call for independence.

In her analysis of the spatial dimensions of the Jaffa protest, Hatuka also observes how the District Commissioner refused to permit a public protest and rejected the demonstration route. In turn, he offered to receive a Palestinian delegation in his office, a plan which itself was rejected by the Palestinian leadership. Hatuka notes that "the British offer to receive a delegation disregarded two key elements of a mass demonstration, namely: the sense of equality achieved by breaking down hierarchal representation, and, secondly, the recognition that a demonstration is a form of inclusion, not reduction as in the case of a small delegation."[90] As a result, the police chief ordered the violent dispersal of the crowd by ordering a baton charge on peaceful protestors.[91] Twenty-one people died and dozens more were injured as a result of police brutality.

Jawhariyyeh shows photographs of police riots in Jaffa and in Jerusalem, where Mandate police are seen beating Palestinians with batons. They are wide shots taken from the roof above the squares, where the photographer can clearly capture that demonstrators are being attacked by the British. Palestinian bodies are on the ground and the police are seen chasing after the large crowd, beating demonstrators indiscriminately. The Jaffa demonstration had a particular emotional meaning for Wasif, as at this event Musa Kazhim al-Husseini, then in his eighties, was beaten by the British so badly that he died from the injuries a few months later. The albums contain photographs of the demonstrations both in Jaffa and Jerusalem, which form a series of images that are intended to speak to one another, just as the photographs of the Arab Women's Executive Committee, in a dynamic way.

FIGURE 5.18. Arab demonstrations protesting Jewish immigration in Jaffa, October 27, 1933. Jawhariyyeh Album 2, IPS Beirut.

The Jerusalem images start with throngs of men pushing, peacefully, through the narrow streets of Bab al-Khalil, who are then surrounded by British gendarmes and then attacked by British police at Bab al-Khalil and Bab al-Jadid (fig. 5.18). The Jerusalem images are followed by similar images of British police, on horse and foot, charging and savagely attacking demonstrators in Jaffa.

These images document more than a sustained pattern and policy of violence and police abuse of Palestinians. Rather, they offer a dissensual history, a latent history that emerges even in Jawhariyyeh's own imaginary museum. These images are not only documents of the lived experiences of the notable class and ruling elite, but also clearly give life to the cross-section of workers, peasants, merchants, and others who filled the streets when the Arab Executive Committee made their official call. Indeed, it is these actors that are largely responsible for dragging the Palestinian leadership, eventually, to support the Great Revolt. Rashid Khalidi suggests that the violence of 1933 was a turning point that gave visibility to the failures, infighting, and, indeed, corruption of the traditional ruling class who had worked with the Zionists and British to suppress a more militant younger generation that began to consider armed struggle.[92]

Jawhariyyeh, perhaps inadvertently, exposes that, despite their colonial civilizational discourses, his employers and rulers, the British, relied on brute violence to repress Palestinian aspirations and, in turn, clearly demonstrated favoritism to the Zionists. The images document the disintegration of an aging Ottoman-era leadership of Palestine, who believed that they could engage Mandate authorities and negotiate themselves into liberation. Many of them, like Jawhariyyeh, worked for the British while also advocating independence. While many decried the Zionist program and its British supporters, they also secretly took money from the Zionists, like Musa Kazhim himself, or sold land to the Zionists at exorbitant profit, like 'Awni 'Abd al-Hadi.[93] Between jockeying for power and for access to capital, the ruling elite were caught within their own rivalries, for example between the Husseinis and the Nashishibis, rivalries that would result in collusion with the British and the Zionists. All the while, the working class and the peasantry—those who worked for or had patron-client relations with the ruling elite—seemed ready and capable of mobilizing on the ground when the political moment demanded.

Jawhariyyeh's images of *muzhaharat*, of manifestations, introduce a "gap in the sensible itself." The images of demonstrations provide a dissensual history that allows us to approach Palestinian resistance without romanticizing it as monolithic. A dissensual history navigates contradictions—the absences of women, peasants and workers with the presence of mass demonstrations, for example. But also, this dissensual history, in the process of identifying contradictions within Palestinian civil and political society, notes them as historical facts determined by multiple vectors of political and social forces within Palestinian lifeworlds; lifeworlds caught in confrontation, negotiation and even collaboration with the power of British colonial authorities and growing Zionist immigration and mobilization. Presenting a series of frenetic, surviving images of demonstrations and their repression provides a method by which the albums reclaim the sensible, reclaim the contradictions and complexities inherent in any political society that are otherwise prohibited by the *partage*/partitions/distribution along colonial settler sensibilities.

The logic of colonialism and the naturalized ideology of settler-colonialism charge us to read these surviving images as relics of a lost past, a tragic un-realized state, and a people on their way to extinction. However, if we translate "surviving images" into Arabic, they will be read as "living images," *suwar m'ayishah*, or perhaps more accurately *suwar hayah*. These images as living images refuse the logics of colonialism, the perspectives of the Orientalist lens, and the ideology of the settler colonial state. To see these surviving images as living images repatriates them to Palestine, repatriates them as "our photography." I myself offer this analysis not as a Palestinian but as a Lebanese Arab sibling and scholar, who is empowered by these living images to reclaim "our" shared history, empowered to refuse the naturalization of the unnatural division of our communities.

Surviving living images of Palestine refuse Sykes-Picot and 1948. In other words, the demand emerging from surviving living images is not a nationalist demand but an epistemological, cultural, and political demand. It demands us to move away from the headlock of the *umheimlich*, the uncanniness of Jawhariyyeh's photographs that draw us to nostalgically imagine a lost and irretrievable Palestinian history. The framework demands us to accept these images as un-partitioned history itself, as undivided sensibilities of social relations of the colonized, as texts that cut across Palestine from pre-1948 to the current moment. Tethering the visual to the political, Rancière states that "politics revolves around what is seen and what can be said about it, around who had the ability to see and the talent to speak around properties of spaces and the possibilities of time."[94] The reference to Rancière is intended only towards the realization of legitimacy at the heart of not only producing photographs, but also deploying them in order to give meaning to one's world, in order, even, to produce one's world as it struggles against being stripped by British colonizers and Zionist settlers.

Therefore, reading Jawhariyyeh's albums through the prism of surviving or living images, settler-colonial logics and settler-colonial futures are disrupted and denaturalized. The effect of Jawhariyyeh's photographs becomes restorative, although not because they "give light" to the "unseen" in the visual. It is restorative, rather, because the albums insist we perceive Palestine as present reality under the brutal forces of Zionist settler-colonialism. The surviving images restore the dissensual reality of Palestinian modernity that exists in an unbroken continuity until today. The centering of the contradictions, tensions, competing forces, desires and interest within Palestinian polity allows us to approach the social, class, gendered, and material contradictions within Palestinian society and history without abrogating Palestinian claims to Palestine. In fact, this approach allows us to evince these claims. Approaching Jawhariyyeh's albums as a consortium of surviving images permits us to critically approach Palestinian history itself as not a byproduct of Zionist determination, British machinations and collusion, and Palestinian failure. Rather, the interplay of images in Jawhariyyeh's albums emancipates Palestinian history from Zionist and colonial narratives. Rather than continuously having to answer questions and statements as framed by the settler-colony and its patrons, this method of reading the interaction between the images decolonizes the Palestinian visual archive and Palestinian history. The decolonial method, then, acknowledges the contradictions and tensions that structure all colonial societies and national movements, which include bourgeois machinations to hijack the national movement, the collusion of the ruling class with settler-colonial forces, and the suppression of the leading role of subaltern classes in the revolutionary struggle. The surviving images that Wasif draws from the Orientalist and expatriate archive and places in his *musée imaginaire palestinien* centers "our photography" of the Palestinians and the undeniable *living* reality of transhistorical Palestine, from the River to the Sea.

6

——

Epilogue

The Presence and Potential of Palestine

A Palestinian prisoner sits on the threshold step of a doorway of, what one might assume to be a jail, surrounded by three British soldiers (fig. 6.1). His name is Karam bin Saba al-Shamma'. We know little about him. We do not know why he is there. We cannot discern what he has in his hands. Is he a political prisoner? Aren't all prisoners under colonial rule political prisoners? We do not know the reasons for the rather informal, over-exposed, vertical photograph, likely taken by an amateur photographer. We only know al-Shamma' because Wasif Jawhariyyeh included this photograph in his albums and told us about him in the albums' index:

> The prisoner Karam bin Saba al-Shamma' is from the Orthodox community in Jerusalem. This young man was brazen and uneducated. Like they say, 'every wedding has a blemish.' He was very active and one of the jail's best clients. His end came when the 1948 Revolution happened. He exited the Old City from Bab al-Jadid (The New Gate) and entered into Atallah Storeroom. Its owner, Lutfi, sold Eastern souvenirs. The violence between the Arabs and the Jews intensified in front of this store and Notre Dame. A bomb hit him and ended his life. Dead, he sat on a chair for the duration of three days. No one was there to save him or pull him from the store.

Jawhariyyeh's explanation of al-Shamma' might suggest the reason why he seems almost as at ease as his captors. Al-Shamma' was a ne'er-do-well, although one that became a martyr, a *shahid*—a term that Jawhariyyeh does not use to describe him. This image and its story are deceptively confusing. Why would Jawhariyyeh, so concerned with men of repute (and they are almost all *men*, in his albums) in Palestine include an image of an urban layabout in jail, not even referencing his martyrdom except in the index? The inclusion of this image tells us much about the organizing logic of the albums itself. Namely, Jawhariyyeh, while desperately faithful to

FIGURE 6.1. Prisoner Karam bin Saba al-Shamma' in "special detention". Jawhariyyeh Album 2, IPS Beirut.

the elite ruling class that he and his father served, could genuinely understand the crisscrossing of various members from particular classes with colonial administrators and functionaries to form the basic social fabric of Jerusalem.

Edward Said's contemplation in *After the Last Sky* about his relationship to a number of different classes in Palestine comes to mind. Perhaps similar in ways to Jawhariyyeh, Said acknowledges that he, as a son and even grandson of "doctors, business people, and professionals," had "no direct personal immediacy" with a "population of poor, suffering, occasionally colorful peasants," who he confesses as having perceived as "unchanging and collective."[1] He realizes that "this perception of mine is mythic . . . (de)formed by the specific inflections of our history and the special circumstance out of which my identity emerged."[2] This self-reflection of a fellow Jerusalemite calls us to think about Jawhariyyeh's own engagement with other classes in Jerusalem, classes and social groups that, as with women, are largely absent from his visual narrative.

As his diaries show us, Jawhariyyeh's social life and activities cut through all strata of Palestinian society. In those pages, he narrates—both as a musician and *a petit-fonctionnaire*—his movement through social and physical spaces that transcend the class divide. Women, too, and his interactions and social relationships with them, are more robustly represented in these diaries, given depth, color, and dimension. Yet, on the surface, Jawhariyyeh's albums represent where the urban political and economic elites, communal and sectarian leadership, and the *effendi* class intersect with Jerusalem and its surroundings as a lived space and Palestine as a society and geographic space under transformation and considerable political challenges. Yet, a closer and more deliberative look at these albums brings to fruition a number of realizations, including that other social actors and players weave themselves in and out of the images. Photography acts as a means to animate the social relations and their narratives, imaginaries, histories and stories, stories that are told and remain untold.

Philip Gourevitch and Errol Morris remind us that photographs themselves "cannot tell stories." However, what they may provide is "evidence of stories," evidence that might be dampened, displaced, repressed or excluded from consideration; evidence in an image where its indexical nature might have been purloined by the colonial eye but awaits liberation from the native inhabitants' experience. Jennifer Tucker allows us to think about Gourevitch and Morris's insights as an interpretative process, where "a photograph can best be understood not as an answer or an end to inquiry, but as an invitation to look more closely, and ask questions."[3] The photograph as evidence, the photograph as document, the photograph as history, the photograph as narrative, the photograph as indeterminant, and the photograph as momentary, all rest on one empirical constant. That is, the photograph is a mark of presence as much as absence and obfuscation. Against the onslaught of negation of Palestinian existence, indeed Palestinian being, this realization underwrites our examination of Jawhariyyeh's photography albums.

POTENTIAL HISTORY, UNDENIABLE PRESENCE

The enigmatic photograph and story of Karam al-Shamma' opens multiple possibilities for reading Jawhariyyeh's albums but also multiple avenues to explore Palestinian existence, life, and culture, not only within a particular historical moment or era but as a sustained, contiguous, and unbroken ontology of Palestine and its inhabitants. The method by which we approach our mapping of the unbroken Palestinian presence in Palestine is to develop a variety of contrapuntal readings that connect spectators throughout time to particular places and fixed moments in Palestinian history. In this sense, we engaged the various ways in which photography broadens our scope of history, but also broadens the very possibilities in which photography and the photographic archive can help us decolonize Palestine.

Our assorted methodologies for exploring the multiple dimensions of photography place Palestine at the center stage of its own history and wrench it away from the Orientalist and Zionist narratives and the concomitant colonial gaze that has dominated the field of "Holy Land" photography since the nineteenth century. This book as a whole denaturalizes Zionist settler-colonial logic and colonialist hegemony by recentering Palestinian lives, but also by reenfranchising these lives with the archive that the "history of Middle Eastern photography" attempts to extract from them. This book and its photographs offer the possibility to envision Palestine without having to "imagine" it as a colonized country. This possibility becomes apparent if we consider what Ariella Azoulay called the "potential history," which is not just history that could have been but the history that "creates new conditions both for the appearance of things and for our appearance as its narrators."[4]

Building upon Walter Benjamin's concept of "incomplete history," Azoulay argues that from our present vantage point, we are able to "render the past potentially reversible." In other words, the act of "watching" photography "entails dimensions of time and movement that need to be reinscribed in the interpretation of the still photographic image."[5] The photographs in Jawahirriyeh's albums, therefore, have the power to re-inscribe—literally, rewrite—the way we understand the temporality and materiality of Palestine. Our various methodologies of approaching the photographic image and archive unambiguously assert the centrality of the indigenous inhabitants of Palestine, while illustrating potentialities in history that tend to be displaced through the violence to which Palestinian society and lives were and are subjected.

At the most fundamental level, the albums present us with the opportunity to de-exceptionalize Palestine, to approach it empirically as a "normal" country that has a past, present, and future with a vibrant society. Certainly, the photographic archive can allow us to understand that Palestine could have developed into an independent country if it had not been derailed by Zionist settler-colonialism.

However, this too may be a misstep in thinking about the full potentiality of looking at photographs from the late Ottoman and Mandate periods; namely, the very concept of Palestine as an independent state arises only with the violations of the Arab body politic by the Sykes-Picot Agreement and the Balfour Declaration. In other words, although we have no pretentions to have initiated the project, we hope that this book contributes to witnessing a Palestine that traverses history and geography and binds individuals, families, and communities to institutions and social formations within Palestine but also that reaches beyond what would have been an independent Republic of Palestine. If nothing else, the images in this book, and Jawhariyyeh's albums in general, enable us to envision a decolonized Palestine and Palestinians outside the hegemonic confines of considering Palestinians as stateless and static victims of trauma, held in suspension since 1948. Instead, the albums present the Palestinians as citizens of their own country, a country not circumscribed by colonial rule or imperialist dictates nor by Zionist colonization but by defined by its own dynamics, histories, coherences, and tensions that cross class, gender, and religious sects as well as intermingle with the polities that are now known as Syrian, Lebanese, Jordanian, and Armenian societies.

The three complementary analytic contributions to *Camera Palæstina* interlock through mapping the contours of the social, political, and economic relations within Palestinian polity and geography. Let us approach one additional image from Jawhariyyeh's albums that illustrates the multiple ways contrapuntal readings emerge from these images. Wasif, as we have seen, spends considerable time on the 1929 Buraq Revolution. He provides three images of an ad hoc Spontaneous Committee for Emergency Aid (*Lijnat al-is'af al-munbathiqah*) that organized during, or at least in the immediate wake, of the revolution. The first image is that of a typical group of besuited, cravated, mustached, and largely un-tarbushed effendis sitting on chairs and a small desk. Jawhariyyeh numbers and, in his index, identifies them: Thabit Khalil Darwish, Fu'ad al-Imam, Safwat Younis al-Husseini, Adel Bey Hassan al-Turjman, the lawyer Hassan Sidqi al-Dajani, Ismail Haqqi al-Nashashibi, the lawyer Subhi Abu Khudr, Ishaq Darwish, and Shakib Musa al-Nashashibi.

Two more images depict the committee members statically posing with "peasants" in villages where the Committee distributed aid. An array of second-tier elites poses in front of the *fellahin* while "distributing aid" in the village of Beit Safafa, a *nahiyah* of Jerusalem (fig. 6.2). The photograph is terribly underexposed, blacking out or making it very difficult to identify the faces of those pictured. But again, Jawhariyyeh provides the identities of these committee members: Tunnas Shalhit, Shakib Musa al-Nashashibi, al-Sheikh Muhammad al-Salih, Khalid Bey al-Duzdar, Muhammad al-Sabasi, Raghib 'Abd al-Qadir al-'Afifi, Ibrahim Isma'il Bey al-Husseini, Thabit Darwish, and Izzat Tannus.

How to read such a static, enigmatic, and poor-quality image? Does it even matter that the image is underexposed? Those that are worthy to be identified, namely the elites, are named. The peasants remain characteristically quiet, anonymous,

FIGURE 6.2. Spontaneous Committee for Emergency Aid, Beit Safafa. Jawhariyyeh Album 2, IPS Beirut.

and unidentifiable. Through the lens of Jawhariyyeh, the figures in the photo were the men of his community with whom he regularly fraternized, served, and interacted. They were notables along with the "new men" of the Empire, as Peter Gran has called them.[6] These were the men of means, access, and capital, as Sherene Seikaly identifies them.[7] None of those pictured are particularly famous, although they each came from notable Jerusalemite families, mostly Muslim. Many of them were moving out of the Old City and building homes in the new suburbs of al-Quds such as Baq'a, Abu Tur, and Musrara. The family names attached to these members reinforces our knowledge of the interconnected social network of mid- and upper-tier elites with one another, but also their ability to organize despite personal and family rivalries. We know that a number of these men were "professionals," likely educated in Palestine's post-*nahdah* educational curriculum. Hassan Sidqi al-Dajani, for example, in the initial image of the Committee, was part of the leadership of the nationalist cultural "club," *al-Muntada al-adabi*, and close to the Nashashibi family. *Al-Muntada*, along with *al-Nadi al-'arabi*, were important youth organizations that galvanized "a new generation of political activists" in Palestine in the immediate aftermath of the First World War.[8]

The Committee's members likely participated in these or similar cultural-political groups. The images allow us to speculate with considerable confidence

that these members could so quickly and efficiently create rather large spontaneous groups that actually could, with equal acuity, distribute aid to the "needy" during the Revolt, not only because they enjoyed social relationships but because they
shared actual organizing experience around nationalist issues. For example, we
know little about Raghib 'Abd al-Qadir al-'Afifi, casually leaning against the wall
of blocks in the present image. Jawhariyyeh mentions al-'Afifi in his diaries as the
supervisor under whom he worked in al-Baladiyah (Jerusalem's municipality). He
looks incredibly similar to Ibrahim Isma'il Bey al-Husseini, next to him. Ibrahim is
likely to be the grandson of Musa al-Husseini, late nineteenth century Jerusalem's
chief magistrate and one of its most powerful businessmen, who was the father-in-
law of an Ottoman Grand Vizier, and father of Ismail and Shukri.[9] While Ibrahim's
father, Ismail, was a respected merchant of the city, his brother Shukri is renowned
as an early nationalist, forming the Arab-Ottoman Brotherhood and becoming
one of the leading political figures in Ottoman Palestine.[10] The photograph is not
only a "document" but also a field of certainty, and indeed materiality, that allows
a "potential history," or perhaps a "more likely history," to emerge. While we may
know little detail about the *Lijnat al-is'af al-munbathiqah* or its members, we are
able to quickly assess a collective fact: namely, the organization of Palestinians
during the Revolt were not capricious or even spontaneous at all, but rather the
result of a sustained political culture of nationalist activism that had been forged
in an intellectual, social, political, and economic network within Palestinian Arab
society since the beginning of the century, if not before.

Finally, a contrapuntal reading also proceeds from other elements of the
photographic image. The most obvious is, of course, that we contrast the relative
anonymity of these notables to the absolute anonymity of the peasants. If we are
able to designate certain histories of the social networks of politics, mobilization,
from the scant information that Jawhariyyeh provides in his albums and index,
we can determine significantly less about those "needy" who are receiving aid.
The opaque composition of the photograph, the indiscernible underexposed faces
of peasants who stand behind the effendis and even the rocks and wall, parallels
Jawhariyyeh's own narrative obfuscation. Yet this does not mean that these men
were marginal. It only means that they were being positioned as the needy "peasants" at a time of the formation of a modern national discourse, as Rana Barakat and Sherene Seikaly have most recently shown.[11] This obfuscation draws us
to think, then, of who these Palestinians were, most notably as connected to their
village Beit Safafa.

Beit Safafa's history is illustrative of the Palestinian experience. A Muslim village on the road between al-Quds and Beit Laham (Bethlehem), the village was
attacked in 1929 by Zionists from the nearby settler colony of Makor Haim, built
only three years before by Polish Jews. Jawhariyyeh himself, it seems, bought a
plot of land adjacent to Makor Haim in 1940.[12] In 1948, the Green Line divided
Beit Safafa, previously "a village of farmers and stone cutters."[13] The village was

captured, colonized, and annexed by the Zionists in 1967, absorbed into metropolitan occupied Jerusalem. Several thousand internally displaced Palestinian "refugees" settled there, some of whom have Israeli citizenship while others have blue ID cards, or "temporary residency" in their own country. The photograph surrenders little to us regarding the social history and lives of the people of Beit Safafa at the time it was taken, but perhaps that is the way that they must maintain their presence in the village. If we can draw such confident speculation about the relationship between Jawhariyyeh's visual narrative as articulating a national bourgeois vision, perhaps we can also extend such an analysis to the rare, and always anonymous, appearance of the *fellah* in these albums. In particular, just as Jawhariyyeh does not provide any information about these Palestinians, we see that the members of the Committee, in their magnanimity of delivering aid, stand explicitly in front of the villagers to block them from the camera. Matching written to visual narrative, we can infer that the complex social networks of notable and rising middle-class families, while undoubtedly interacting with them on a daily basis, actively sought to overshadow, block, and obfuscate the presence of working and peasant-class Palestinians from a national narrative.

If the 1929 Revolt was initiated and largely led by peasants and "villagers"—those from villages within Greater Jerusalem—it is also important to highlight how the Palestinian ruling class initially disavowed and steered away from the violence.[14] The approaches in this book seek not only to break from the gravitational orbit of Zionism and British colonialism as the determining forces of Palestinian life, but also to interrogate and make visible the class, sectarian, and gender forces that, as in the case of this image, literally stand in the way of us seeing the Palestinian working and peasant classes, which include the expropriated and wage labor of women.

CENTERING PALESTINIANS

Some twenty-five years ago, Beshara Doumani, in his groundbreaking *Rediscovering Palestine*, "wonder[ed]" out loud "how it is possible to underhand the social structure, cultural life, and economic development of Palestinian society during the Mandate" in the absence of sustained scholarship on the period.[15] The Mandate is finally enjoying increasing and well-deserved scholarly attention.[16] What is most important about this attention is that it seeks, like Doumani's work, to emerge from the confines of a paradigm demarcated by ascribed binaries of Arab nationalism versus Ottomanism, Palestinians as nationalist exceptions versus Palestinians as Arab nationalists, Zionist settlers and British colonial rulers as determinative of Palestinian identity, and Palestinian identity as a construct or effect of the politics of notables. Indeed, these paradigms emerge not only directly from the tenacious legacies and afterlives of Orientalism as a regime of analysis, but also the epistemology of modernity itself (Arab modernity included).

Rana Barakat's work has not emerged in this conclusion by coincidence. It appears as perhaps an articulate representation of the current state and direction of Palestinian Studies. The work cited here represents an impressive wave of recent studies that carefully, rigorously, and daringly center Palestinian history as a history that is not exclusively defined in relation to Zionism and British colonialism but in relation to the continuity of Palestinian life, social networks, political formations, and economic formations over more than a century, rooted in historic Palestine but also maintained in exile and the "diaspora." In some ways, this method of history writing has been around since the 1960s. Acknowledging Palestinian history as a history of the indigenous people of Palestine, Barakat articulates something that has bound these Palestinian scholars over recent decades. Namely, she insists on "elevating Palestinian indigenous experiences and narrative" as central to the analytic, not always in dialogue or relation to Zionism and colonialism but within its own framework that arises from social, political and economic dynamics of Palestine Arab modernity.[17] Indeed, she is not stating that the Zionist settler existence and British colonial rule are not relevant. Rather, she points to how "the hegemonic presence of the settler on the land is again mirrored as a hegemony embedded within the primary placement of the settler in scholarly literature."[18] The current wave of scholarship, including this book, radically returns to a paradigm of Palestinian Arab history writing that implicitly understands that "indigeneity is a political category."[19]

Camera Palæstina, then, follows in the venerable Arab and Palestinian tradition of seeking means and methods to decolonization. In the case of Jawhariyyeh, each photograph in the album has a life of its own due not only to what it depicts, but as enhanced by the stories Wasif narrates in captions, or in the description provided both in his notebooks and memoirs. Their historical significance is amplified, for not only do we have images from the period, but also commentary. Of course, placing the images and the commentary within the historical context, as well as the context of our times as readers/viewers, increases their significance as sources, as socio-political and historical documents. The albums are situated in various times: that of the capturing of each image; of collecting them in albums; and of the modern history of Palestine, from Ottoman rule to Arab aspirations for collective independence to the formalization of Zionist colonization of Palestine to the current moment.

Still, this book aspires to be more than just a work on an individual collector or a "window into the history" of Palestine. We see it instead as an attempt to elaborate on the various possibilities that photography could provide scholars of colonialism and theoreticians of the postcolonial condition. While our use of photographs is clearly based on their role as evidence that can enhance our study of history, we offer that photographs are more than merely "historical documents."

In the analytic process of contributing to a social history of the Mandate period, we simultaneously never lose awareness of the multiple dimensions and temporalities that are presented by photography, perhaps uniquely so. In handling photographs that commute throughout time, we also highlight how they exist within multiple temporalities (that of their production, their display and exchange, their circulation, and their afterlives and survival). To be blunt, our engagement with Jawhariyyeh's redeployment of commercial photographs intends to conjure a social life that has currency today. Such a séance of meaning and life interrupts the settler-colonial logic of Zionism that seeks to eliminate and replace the Palestinians in the lived geography of Palestine. Therefore, Jawhariyyeh—who is neither hero or anti-hero—gives us albums, often in the most banal form, in order to call us to not only witness but attest. This book stands as such as an attestation; an attestation that Palestine *exists today* just as Palestinians exist today. These albums, whether as testimonial (*shahadah*) or kawshun, attest to the undeniable, material reality of Palestine as an uninterrupted, albeit traumatic and violent, history of presence in a land that belongs to the Palestinian people and a land to which they belong.

NOTES

1. WAYS OF SEEING THE PALESTINIAN VISUAL ARCHIVE

1. Salim Tamari, "Jerusalem's Ottoman Modernity: The Time and Lives of Wasif Jawhariyyeh," *Jerusalem Quarterly* 1 (Summer 2000): 1–34; Stephen Sheehi, *Arab Imago: A Social History of Photographic Portraiture 1850–1920* (Princeton, NJ: Princeton University Press, 2016); Stephen Sheehi, "Portrait Paths: Studio Photography in Ottoman Palestine," *Jerusalem Quarterly* 61 (2015): 23–41; Walid Khalidi, *Before Their Diaspora: A Photographic History of the Palestinians 1876–1948* (Washington, DC: Institute for Palestine Studies, 1984).

2. For the manifesto of the PLO Film Unit and an illuminating discussion of it see Kay Dickenson, *Arab Film and Video Manifestos: Forty-Five Years of the Moving Image Amid Revolution* (New York: Palgrave, 2018), 81–104.

3. For example, see Ali Behdad, *Camera Orientalis: Reflections on Photography of the Middle East* (Chicago: University of Chicago Press, 2016); Issam Nassar, *Laqatat Mughayirah: al-taswir al-fotoghraphi al-mubakkir fi Falastin* (Ramallah: Kutub and Qattan Foundation, 2005); Carmen Perez-Gonzalez, *Local Portraiture: Through the Lens of the 19th Century Iranian Photographers* (Leiden: Leiden University Press, 2012); Markus Ritter and Staci Scheiwiller, eds., *Indigenous Lens: Early Photography in the Near and Middle East* (Berlin: De Gruyter, 2018); Yasmeen Nachabe Taan, *Reading Marie al-Khazen's Photographs: Gender, Photography, Mandate Lebanon* (London: Bloomsbury, 2020); Sheehi, *Arab Imago*.

4. For a contrapuntal history of photography in Southwest Asia that centers indigenous practice, see Stephen Sheehi, "Beyond Orientalism: Toward a History of *Indigenista* Photography in the Arab World," *The Handbook of Photography Studies*, ed. Gil Paternak (London: Bloomsbury, 2020), 353–68.

5. For general information on Yasayi Garabedian and the centrality of Armenians in the photographic history in the Middle East, see Badr el-Hage, "The Armenian Pioneers of Middle Eastern Photography," *Jerusalem Quarterly* 31 (2007): 22–26.

6. Issam Nassar, "Familial Snapshots: Representing Palestine in the Work of the First Local Photographers," *History & Memory* 18, no. 2 (Fall/Winter 2006): 145.

7. Nassar, "Familial Snapshots," 26.

8. The relationship between photography, exoticism of the Holy Land, and postcards has been discussed at length by a number of scholars. One example is Annelies Moors, "Presenting Palestine's Population Premonitions of the Nakba," *MIT Electronic Journal of Middle East Studies* 1 (May 2001): 1–12; Annalies Moors, "Presenting People: The Politics of Picture Postcards of Palestine/Israel," in *Postcards: Ephemeral Histories of Modernity*, ed. David Prochaska and Jordana Mendelson (University Park, PA: Pennsylvania State University Press, 2010), 93–105.

9. For more about the Saboungis, see Sheehi, *Arab Imago*.

10. Mia Gröndahl, *The Dream of Jerusalem: Lewis Larsson and the American Colony Photographers* (Stockholm: Journal, 2006); Barbara Blair, "The American Colony Photography Department: Western Consumption and 'Insider' Commercial Photography," *Jerusalem Quarterly* 44 (2010): 28–38. For a history of the Albina Brothers, see Iris Albina, "Souvenir From Gethsemane: Portrait of the Albina Brothers," *Jerusalem Quarterly* 60 (Autumn 2014): 59–76.

11. See Issam Nassar, "A Jerusalem Photographer: The Life and Work of Hanna Safieh," *Jerusalem Quarterly* 7 (2000): 25. Hanna Safieh also wrote an autobiography, published as *A Man and His Camera: Photographs of Palestine* (Jerusalem: s.n. [Raffi Safieh], 1999).

12. For a few studies on the rising of the *effendiyah* class, see Toufoul Abou Hodeib, *A Taste of Home: The Modern Middle Class in Ottoman Beirut* (Stanford, CA: Stanford University Press, 2017); Beshara Doumani, *Rediscovering Palestine: Merchants and Peasants in Jabal Nablus 1700–1900* (Berkeley: University of California Press, 1995); Wilson Chacko Jacob, *Working Out Egypt: Effendi Masculinity and Subject Formation in Colonial Modernity 1870–1940* (Durham, NC: Duke University Press, 2011).

13. Sherene Seikaly, *Men of Capital: Scarcity and Economy in Mandate Palestine* (Stanford, CA: Stanford University Press, 2016).

14. Seikaly, *Men of Capital*, 13.

15. See Edward J. Erickson, *Ordered to Die: A History of the Ottoman Army in the First World War* (Westport, CT: Greenwood Publishing, 2001), 211; James Gelvin, *The Israel-Palestine Conflict: One Hundred Years of War* (Cambridge, UK: Cambridge University Press, 2005), 77.

16. For a recent complex study of social, economic and political dynamic around the famine, see Melanie Tanielian, *The Charity of War: Famine, Humanitarian Aid and World War I in the Middle East* (Stanford, CA: Stanford University Press, 2017).

17. Seikaly, *Men of Capital*.

18. For a recent study convincingly showing that the success of Zionism and Israel itself is inextricably due to the unwavering political, military, and economic support of sponsoring powers, particularly the British and then Americans, see Rashid Khalidi, *The Hundred Years' War on Palestine: A History of Settler Colonialism and Resistance, 1917–2017* (New York: Metropolitan, 2020).

19. For further discussion of Nicola Saig's "Caliph Umar at Jerusalem's Gates," see Kamal Boullata, *Palestinian Art: 1850 to the Present* (London: Saqi, 2009), 114–16.

20. For more on this painting and allegory, see Stephen Sheehi, "Before Painting: Niqula Saig and Photographic Vision," in *Arab Art Histories: Khaled Shouman Collection (Qira'at fil-fann al-'arabi)* (Amman: Darat al-Funun and Amsterdam: Idea Books, 2014), 361–74.

21. Laura Robson, *Colonialism and Christianity in Mandate Palestine* (Austin: University of Texas Press, 2011); Michelle Campos, *Ottoman Brothers: Muslims, Christians, and Jews in Early Twentieth Century Palestine* (Stanford, CA: Stanford University Press, 2011).

22. See Michael Allen, *In The Shadow of World Literature: Sites of Reading in Colonial Egypt* (Princeton, NJ: Princeton University Press, 2016); Elliot Colla, *Conflicted Antiquities: Egyptology, Egyptomania, Egyptian Modernity* (Durham, NC: Duke University Press, 2008); Tarek El-Ariss, *Trials of Arab Modernity: Literary Effects and the New Political* (New York: Fordham University Press, 2013); Elizabeth Holt, *Fictitious Capital: Silk, Cotton, and the Rise of the Arabic Novel* (New York: Fordham University Press, 2017); Ilham Khuri-Makdisi. *The Eastern Mediterranean and the Making of Global Radicalism, 1860–1914* (Berkeley: University of California Press, 2010); Kamran Rastegar, *Literary Modernity between the Middle East and Europe* (London: Routledge, 2007); Jeff Sacks, *Iterations of Loss* (New York: Fordham University Press, 2015); Samah Selim, *The Novel and Rural Imaginary 1880–1985* (New York: Routledge/Curzon, 2004); Stephen Sheehi, *The Foundations of Modern Arab Identity* (Gainesville: University Press of Florida, 2004); and Shaden Tageldin, *Disarming Words: Empire and the Seduction of Translation in Egypt* (Berkeley: University of California Press, 2011).

23. Lauren Banko, *The Invention of Palestinian Citizenship, 1918–1947* (Edinburgh: University of Edinburgh Press, 2017).

24. For the theory of photography as contract with which this book engages directly and indirectly, see Ariella Aïsha Azoulay, *The Civil Contract of Photography* (New York: Verso, 2012). For some discussion of political thought and concepts of citizenship and political rights of subjects, see Amal Ghazal, *Islamic Reform and Arab Nationalism: Expanding the Crescent from the Mediterranean to the Indian Ocean 1880s–1930s* (London: Routledge, 2010); or Armando Salvatore, *Islam and Political Discourse of Modernity* (Reading: Ithaca Press, 1997); or, for a more micro study of a formative Arab political thinker in terms, see Stephen Sheehi, "Al-Kawakibi: From Political Journalism to a Political Science of the "Liberal" Arab Muslim," *Alif* 37 (2017): 85–109.

25. Cyrus Schayegh, "The Mandates and/as Decolonization," in *The Routledge Handbook of the History of Middle East Mandates*, ed. Cyrus Schayegh and Andrew Arsan (New York: Routledge, 2015): 412.

26. Schayegh, "The Mandates and/as Decolonization," 412.

27. Schayegh, "The Mandates and/as Decolonization," 414.

28. Anibal Quijano, "Colonially of Power, Eurocentrism, and Latin America," *Nepantla: Views from the South* 1, no. 3 (2000): 533–80; Anibal Quijano, "Colonially and Modernity/Rationality," *Cultural Studies* 21, no. 2–3 (March-May 2007): 168–78.

29. Marianne Hirsch, *Family Frames: Photography, Narrative, and Postmemory* (Cambridge, MA: Harvard University Press, 1997).

2. THE ARCHIVAL AND NARRATIVE NATURE OF THE PHOTOGRAPHIC ALBUMS OF WASIF JAWHARIYYEH

1. Jacques Derrida, "Archive Fever: A Freudian Impression," trans. Eric Prenowitz, *Diacritics* 25, no. 2 (Summer, 1995): 9–10.

2. For further discussion of the subject of captions, see John Berger, *Understanding a Photograph* (New York: Penguin, 2013).

3. Bertha Spafford Vester, *Our Jerusalem: An American Family in the Holy City, 1881–1949* (Garden City, NJ: Doubleday and Company Inc., 1950), 256.

4. Wasif Jawhariyyeh, *The Storyteller of Jerusalem: The Life and Times of Wasif Jawhariyyeh, 1904–1948*, ed. Salim Tamari and Issam Nassar, trans. Nada Elzeer (Northampton, MA: Olive Branch Press, 2014), 100.

5. Jawhariyyeh, *Storyteller of Jerusalem*, 99.

6. Jawhariyyeh, *Storyteller of Jerusalem*, 35.

7. Jawhariyyeh, *Storyteller of Jerusalem*, 199.

8. Damian I (July 10, 1848–August 14, 1931) was the Greek Orthodox Patriarch of Jerusalem from 1897 to 1931.

9. On the Ottoman air force, see https://www.globalsecurity.org/military/world/europe/ot-air-history-2.htm.

10. Jawhariyyeh, *Storyteller of Jerusalem*, 95.

11. Jawhariyyeh, *Storyteller of Jerusalem*, 100.

12. Benedict Anderson, *Imagined Communities: Reflections on the Origins and Spread of Nationalism* (London and New York: Verso, 1991), 24.

13. Jawhariyyeh, *Storyteller of Jerusalem*, 222. Ze'ev Jabotinsky was a revisionist Zionist leader in Palestine, who immigrated from Russia and formed a number of extremist right-wing Zionist paramilitary groups, including the infamous Irgun organization.

14. Tahiya Carioca, or Karioka (1915–99) was an Egyptian belly dancer and actress. Badi'a Masabni (1892–1974) was a Syrio-Lebanese belly dancer in Egypt. Farid al-Atrash (1910–74), a Syrian active in Egypt, was a composer, singer, and oud player. Amin Hassanayn was an Egyptian singer most famous for his songs during World War II. Sami al-Shawa (1889–1965) was the most famous Egyptian violinist of the twentieth century. His family came to Egypt from Aleppo in Syria. 'Ali al-Kassar (1887–1957) was a famous Egyptian movie star. 'Umar al-Batsh (1885–1950) was a composer and oud player from Aleppo; he was Wasif's oud instructor and companion during World War I. See Muhammad Sawi, *Tahiyah Kariyuka: ashhar raqisat al-cinema al-misriyah* (*Tahiya Carioca: The Most Famous Dancer of Egyptian Cinema*) (Beirut: Dar al-ratib al-jama'iyah, 1995) and, in English, Sharifa Zuhur, *Colors of Enchantment: Theater, Dance, Music, and the Visual Arts of the Middle East* (Cairo: American University in Cairo Press, 2001).

15. Jawhariyyeh, *Storyteller of Jerusalem*, 179.

16. Mohammad 'Ali Jawhar (1878–1931) was an Indian Muslim activist, journalist and poet whose name is associated with the Khilafat movement.

17. All references to Emile Habibi's novel come from the original Arabic version *al-Waqa' al-gharibah fi ikhtifa' Sa'id Abu al-Nahs al-mutasha'il* (Beirut: Ibn Khaldun for Publishing and Distribution, 1974). However, the book appeared in English translation as *The Secret Life of Saeed: The Pessoptimist*, trans. Trevor LeGassick (Northampton, MA: Interlink Pub Group, 2001). The quotation above is from the Arabic version, page 37.

18. Habibi, *al-Waqaʾ al-Gharibah*, 17.

19. Jawhariyyeh, *The Storyteller of Jerusalem*, 74.

3. VISUAL INTERLUDE: PHOTOGRAPHIC IMAGES FROM OTTOMAN AND MANDATE PALESTINE

1. Stephen Sheehi, "Behind Every Male Photographer: The Invisible History of Arab Women Photographers," *Aramco Magazine* (March–April, 2019): 28–30, https://www.aram coworld.com/en-US/Articles/March-2019/Women-Behind-the-Lens.

2. Silvia Federici, *Revolution at Point Zero: Housework, Reproduction, and Feminist Struggle* (Oakland, CA: PM Press, 2012), 31.

3. For examples of methodologies and strategies that locate the affective experiences as a critical point of departure, see Elspeth H. Brown and Thy Phu, *Feeling Photography* (Durham, NC: Duke University Press, 2014); Tina Campt, *Listening to Images* (Durham, NC: Duke University Press, 2017); and Tina Campt, *Image Matters: Archive, Photography, and the African Diaspora in Europe* (Durham, NC: Duke University Press, 2012).

4. PATRONAGE AND PHOTOGRAPHY: HUSSEIN HASHIM'S MELANCHOLIC JOURNEY

1. Susan Sontag, "Melancholy Objects," in *On Photography* (London: Penguin, 2008), 44.

2. Sontag, "Melancholy Objects," 62–66.

3. J.W. Dewdney, "Melancholy Objects: Notes 'On Photography,'" *C4 Contemporary Art*, n.d., https://c4gallery.com/pedagogy/Sontag-on-Photography-%20essay.html, accessed July 30, 2018.

4. Wasif Jawhariyyeh Photographic Index, Album 2, "Women's Protest, 1929" Images J2/60–169 to J2/61–175.

5. Wasif Jawhariyyeh, Salim Tamari, and Issam Nassar, *al-Quds al-ʿUthmaniyah fil-mudhakkirat al-Jawhariyah: al-kitab al-awwal min mudhakkirat al-musiqi Waṣif Jawhariyah, 1904–1917* (al-Quds: Muʾassasat al-Dirasat al-Maqdisiyah, 2003), 6.

6. Jawhariyyeh, Tamari, and Nassar, *al-Quds al-ʾUthmaniyah*, 6.

7. See a description of the collection in Wasif Jawhariyyeh, *The Storyteller of Jerusalem: The Life and Times of Wasif Jawhariyyeh, 1904–1948*, ed. Salim Tamari and Issam Nassar, trans. Nada Elzeer (Northampton, MA: Olive Branch Press, 2014), 171–73.

8. Guy Debord, *Society of the Spectacle*, trans. Ken Knabb (Berkeley, CA: Bureau of Public Secrets, Public Domain, 2014).

9. Debord, *Society of the Spectacle*, 18.

10. Phil Carney, "Crime, Punishment and the Force of Photographic Spectacle," in *Framing Crime: Cultural Criminology and the Image*, ed. K.J. Hayward and M. Presdee (London: Routledge, 2010), 29.

11. Carney, "Crime, Punishment," 20.

12. Salim Tamari, "The War Photography of Khalil Raad: Ottoman Modernity and the Biblical Gaze," *The Jerusalem Quarterly* 52 (2014): 25–37.

13. I have used here *Al-Quds al-ʾUthmaniyah* and the abridged English version *Storyteller of Jerusalem*.

14. The filming of this event is recorded in Ihsan Turjman's diary, *'Am al-Jarad (Year of the Locust)*. The best photographic image of the launching comes from the École Biblique World War 1 photographic collection, which is reproduced here by permission.

15. Another *taqtuqah, al-Kursannah wal-Ful* ("Homage to Double Book-Keeping") is cited by Jawhariyyeh in the second volume of his memoirs, but no music of this ditty has survived (for the its text see Wasif Jawhariyyeh, ms. 164).

16. Wasif's *Musical Notebook* is a repertoire of Arabic musical collections that were performed in Jerusalem and Palestine at the turn of the century. See *Al-Safina—the Musical Notebooks of Wasif Jawhariyyeh*, unpublished manuscript, IPS Archives, Ramallah.

17. Jawhariyyeh, *Storyteller of Jerusalem*, 62.

18. Nermin Menemencioglu, "The Ottoman Theatre 1839–1923," *Bulletin of the British Society for Middle Eastern Studies* 10, no. 1 (1983): 55–56.

19. Jawhariyyeh, Tamari, and Nassar, *Al-Quds al-'Uthmaniyah*, 133–34.

20. Jawhariyyeh, *Storyteller of Jerusalem*, 79.

21. Cyrus 'Ali Zargar, "The Satiric Method of Ibn Daniyal: Morality and Anti-Morality," *Journal of Arabic Literature* 37, no. 1 (2006): 68–108.

22. Dror Ze'evi, "Hiding Sexuality: The Disappearance of Sexual Discourse in the Late Ottoman Middle East," *The International Journal of Social and Cultural Practice* 49, no. 2 (Summer 2005): 40–41.

23. Ze'evi, "Hiding Sexuality," 40.

24. 'Ali Hasan Bawab, *Mawsu'at Yafa al-Jamilah*, Vol. 2 (Beirut: al-Mu'assasa al-'Arabi yalid-Dirasat wal-Nasr, 2003): 1519–20.

25. Ze'evi, "Hiding Sexuality," 42. For a discussion of the origins of Karagoz and Hacivat see https://en.wikipedia.org/wiki/Karagöz_and_Hacivat, accessed October 19, 2020. The text of the Jerusalem performances of Karakoz and Uwaz can be reviewed in Jawhariyyeh, Tamari, and Nassar, *al-Quds al-'Uthmaniyah*, 82–88

26. Jawhariyyeh, Tamari, and Nassar, *al-Quds al-'Uthmaniyah*, 88.

27. Jawhariyyeh, Tamari, and Nassar, *al-Quds al-'Uthmaniyah*, 79–88.

28. Jawhariyyeh, Tamari, and Nassar, *al-Quds al-'Uthmaniyah*, 81.

29. Jawhariyyeh, Tamari, and Nassar, *al-Quds al-'Uthmaniyah*, 80.

30. Jawhariyyeh, Tamari, and Nassar, *al-Quds al-'Uthmaniyah*, 81. The Hindiyah Café still exists opposite Damascus Café, a century later, and has now been converted into a fast food restaurant (2017).

31. Jawhariyyeh, Tamari, and Nassar, *al-Quds al-'Uthmaniyah*, 130.

32. Samir Franciscus, "Palestine 1896 short film (La Palestina en 1896) by the Lumiere Brothers," https://www.youtube.com/watch?v = OxemkAXlr8s, accessed September 21, 2020.

33. Douglas Knoop, *Colour Impression: Report to the Albert Kahn Trustees on the Results of a Journey Round the World, July 21, 1913, to July 24, 1914* ([SP.]: Forgotten Books, 2016).

34. Jawhariyyeh, Tamari, and Nassar, *al-Quds al-'Uthmaniyah*, 130; Jawhariyyeh, *Storyteller of Jerusalem*, 62.

35. Jawhariyyeh, *Storyteller of Jerusalem*, 176.

36. Jawhariyyeh, *Storyteller of Jerusalem*, 91, 204.

37. Jawhariyyeh, *Storyteller of Jerusalem*, 178.

38. Jawhariyyeh, *Storyteller of Jerusalem*, 178–19.

39. Adil Manna, *A 'lam Filastin fi awakhir al-'ahd al-'Uthmani (1800–1918)* (Beirut, Institute for Palestine Studies, 2008), 121–24.

40. Manna, *A 'lam Filastin*, 124–30.

41. Jawhariyyeh, *Storyteller of Jerusalem*, 27.

42. Jawhariyyeh, *Storyteller of Jerusalem*, 22.

43. Jawhariyyeh, *Storyteller of Jerusalem*, 25.

44. Jawhariyyeh, *Storyteller of Jerusalem*, 11.

45. Mana, *'Alam*,121; Jawhariyyeh, *Storyteller of Jerusalem*, 23.

46. Jawhariyyeh, *Storyteller of Jerusalem*, 23.

47. Jawhariyyeh, Tamari, and Nassar, *al-Quds al-'Uthmaniyah*, 139; Jawhariyyeh, *Storyteller of Jerusalem*, 24.

48. Salim Tamari, *Year of the Locust: A Soldier's Diary and the Erasure of Palestine's Ottoman Past* (Berkeley: University of California Press, 2015), 111–12.

49. Jawhariyyeh, *Storyteller of Jerusalem*, 173. Turjman also discusses widespread prostitution in Jerusalem during the war. See Tamari, *Year of the Locust*, 65.

50. Knoop, *Colour Impressions*.

51. Jawhariyyeh, *Storyteller of Jerusalem*, 38.

52. Jawhariyyeh, *Storyteller of Jerusalem*, 39, 63, 272.

53. Sontag, "Melancholy Objects," 41, 44, 54. See also a short reflection by a student identified only as "j2lajoie," "Mourning the Real through Photography," https://selfierhetoric .net/2015/01/22/mourning-the-real-through-photography-a-brief-summary-of-sontags-melancholy-objects, accessed July 28, 2020.

54. Manna, *'Alam*, 123. The sewage system was never realized during Husseini's tenure, for lack of funding, and was soon canceled by the onset of the war.

55. Vivian Gilbert, *The Romance of the Last Crusade: With Allenby to Jerusalem* (New York [u.a.]: Appleton-Century, 1939), 154–70.

56. Gilbert, *The Romance of the Last Crusade*, 166.

57. Gilbert, *The Romance of the Last Crusade*, 167.

58. Jawhariyyeh, Tamari, and Nassar, *al-Quds al-'Uthmaniyah*, 254.

59. Jawhariyyeh, Tamari, and Nassar, *al-Quds al-'Uthmaniyah*, 256. The date is according to the Ottoman mali calendar. The actual years of Ottoman administration were 414 hijra years.

60. Jawhariyyeh, Tamari, and Nassar, *al-Quds al-'Uthmaniyah*, 255.

61. Wasif Jawhariyyeh, Salim Tamari, and Issam Nassar, *al-Quds al-Intidabiyah fil-mudhakkirat al-Jawhariyah: al-kitab al-awwal min mudhakkirat al-musiqi Wasif Jawhariyah, 1904–1917* (al-Quds: Mu'assasat al-Dirasat al-Maqdisiyah, 2003), 277.

62. Jawhariyyeh, Tamari, and Nassar, *al-Quds al-Intidabiyah*, 278.

63. Jawhariyyeh, Tamari, and Nassar, *al-Quds al-Intidabiyah*, 279 .

64. Jawhariyyeh, Tamari, and Nassar, *al-Quds al-'Uthmaniyah*, 180. This episode refers to his father's memory of the closure of the city's walls after sunset—he mentions the year 1845—"when I was a boy in Harat al-Sa'diyah."

65. *al-Safina*, musical notebook of Wasif Jawhariyyeh (undated manuscript), IPS Archives, Ramallah.

66. Jawhariyyeh, *Storyteller of Jerusalem*, xxiii; Jawhariyyeh, Tamari, and Nassar, *al-Quds al-'Uthmaniyah*, 175.

67. Kirsten Seale, "Eye-Swiping London: Iain Sinclair, Photography and the *Flâneur*," *Literary London: Interdisciplinary Studies in the Representation of London* 3, no. 2 (September 2005), http://www.literarylondon.org/london-journal/september2005/seale.html.

68. See Salim Tamari, "City of Riffraff: Crowds, Public Space, and New Urban Sensibilities in War-Time Jerusalem, 1917–1921," in *Comparing Cities: The Middle East and South Asia*, ed. Kamran Asdar 'Ali and Martina Rieker (Oxford: Oxford University Press, 2010).

5. OUR PHOTOGRAPHY: REFUSING THE 1948 PARTITION OF THE SENSIBLE

1. For a recent critical overview of the "history of Middle East photography," locating the "Orientalist" and "expatriate" traditions of photography of the Middle East in relation to the history of indigenous (Arab and Armenian) photography of the Middle East, see Stephen Sheehi, "Beyond Orientalism: Toward a History of Indigenista Photography in the Arab World," in *The Handbook of Photography Studies*, ed. Gil Pasternak (London: Bloomsbury, 2020), 353–68. Also see Sheehi, *Arab Imago*, and Ali Behdad, *Camera Orientalis: Reflections on Photography of the Middle East* (Chicago: University of Chicago Press, 2016), which offers a complex re-reading of Orientalist photography and its circulation and deployment in the Middle East.

2. Rashid Khalidi, *Palestinian Identity: The Construction of Modern National Consciousness* (New York: Columbia University Press, 2010), 46.

3. Khalidi, *Palestinian Identity*, 43.

4. Khalidi, *Palestinian Identity*, 54.

5. The image appears on the Khalidi Library webpage, where all the members are identified. See http://www.khalidilibrary.org/opening.html.

6. Patrick Cabral, *Amílcar Cabral: Revolutionary Leadership and People's War* (Cambridge, UK: Cambridge University Press, 1983), 172 (my italics).

7. Jacques Rancière, *Politics of Aesthetics: Distribution of the Sensible*, trans. Gabriel Rockhill (London: Continuum, 2004), 14.

8. Khalidi, *Palestinian Identity*, 45.

9. Khalidi, *Palestinian Identity*, 46.

10. Some have asserted that Ottoman photographic practice intentionally pushed back against Orientalist representations; see Zeynep Çelik, "Speaking Back to Orientalist Discourse at the World's Columbian Exposition," in *Noble Dreams, Wicked Pleasures: Orientalism in America 1870–1930*, ed. Holly Edwards (Princeton, NJ: Princeton University Press, 2000).

11. David Scott, *Conscripts of Modernity: The Tragedy of Colonial Enlightenment* (Durham, NC: Duke University Press, 2004).

12. For an enlightening study about how European powers regularly thought in terms of partitions and population transfers as viable political solutions to "ethnic" conflicts that were fueled, in fact, through European design (for example, patronizing and favoring some communities over others to curry allies and stoke division), see Laura Robson, *States of Separation: Transfer, Partition and the Making of the Modern Middle East* (Berkeley: University of California Press, 2017).

13. Georges Didi-Huberman, *The Surviving Image: Phantoms of Time and Time of Phantoms: Aby Warburg's History of Art*, trans. Harvey Mendelsohn (University Park, PA: Pennsylvania State University, 2017), 48.

14. Didi-Huberman, *The Surviving Image*, 37.

15. The diary has been published in full in Arabic in two volumes: Wasif Jawhariyyeh, *al-Quds al-'uthmaniyah fil-mudhakkirat al-Jawhariyyeh: al-Kitab al-awal min al-musiqi Wasif Jawhariyyeh 1904–1917*, ed. Salim Tamari and Issam Nassar (Beirut: Mu'assasah al-dirasat al-Filastiniyah, 2003) and Wasif Jawhariyyeh, *al-Quds al-intidabiyah fil-mudhakkirat al-Jawhariyah: al-Kitab al-thani min al-musiqi Wasif Jawhariyah 1918–1948*, ed. Salim Tamari and Issam Nassar (Beirut: Mu'assasah al-dirasat al-Filastiniyah, 2005). Unless otherwise noted, most English translations are taken from the English edition of Jawhariyyeh's diary, *The Storyteller of Jerusalem: The Life and Times of Wasif Jawhariyyeh, 1904–1948*, ed. Salim Tamari and Issam Nassar, trans. Nada Elzeer (Northampton, MA: Olive Branch Press, 2014). For an introduction to Jawhariyyeh, see Salim Tamari, "Jerusalem's Ottoman Modernity: The Time and Lives of Wasif Jawhariyyeh," *Jerusalem Quarterly* 1 (Summer 2000): 1–34.

16. See Nadera Shalhoub Kevorkian, "Palestinian Women and the Politics of Invisibility: Towards a Feminist Methodology," *Peace Prints: South Asian Journal of Peacebuilding* 3, no. 1 (Spring 2010): 1–21; Andreas Hackl, "Immersive Invisibility in the Settler-Colonial City: The Conditional Inclusion of Palestinians in Tel Aviv," *American Ethnologist* 45, no. 3 (2018): 1–13; and Ilana Feldman, "Refusing Invisibility: Documentation and Memorialization in Palestinian Refugee Claims," *Journal of Refugee Studies* 21 (2008): 498–516.

17. Nadera Shalhoub-Kevorkian, "Speaking Life, Speaking Death: Jerusalemite Children Confronting Israel's Technologies of Violence," in *The Emerald Handbook of Feminism, Criminology and Social Change*, ed. Sandra Walklate et al (London: Emerald Publishing Limited, 2020): 253–70.

18. For thinking about a method for "decolonizing" the colonial archive and making the invisible visible, see Stephen Sheehi, "Searching for a Method in a Plate of Hummus: Reading Photographs from Mandate Palestine," in *Imaging and Imagining Palestine: Photography, Modernity, and the Biblical Lens 1818–1948*, ed. Karéne Sanchez Summer and Sary Zananiri (Leiden: Brill, 2021), 346–65.

19. Gil Hochberg, *Visual Occupations: Violence and Visibility in a Conflict Zone* (Durham, NC: Duke University Press, 2015). Hochberg's work is in conversation with Nicholas Mirzoeff, *Rights to Look: A Counter History of Visuality* (Durham, NC: Duke University Press, 2011). The issue of race, in particular blackness, in the United States also seems to be instructive in thinking about the "value" of blackness as always in relation to whiteness or "visibility." See, for an example of such an inquiry, Charles W. Mills, *Blackness Visible: Essays on Philosophy and Race* (Ithaca, NY: Cornell University Press, 2015).

20. Sara Ahmed, *Queer Phenomenology: Orientations, Objects, Others* (Durham, NC: Duke University Press, 2006).

21. Ahmed, *Queer Phenomenology*, 170.

22. Geoffrey Batchen, *Each Wild Idea: Writing, Photography, History* (Cambridge, MA: MIT Press, 2000), 60.

23. A number of important publications push us to think about the intersection between ableism and visuality. While few have specifically engaged in confronting not only the metaphor but the epistemological prism of "visuality," a number of important works reach beyond physical dimensions of ableism and capacity and the ways in which representation colludes with ableism even when unintended, including in regards to photography. See, for example, Benjamin Fraser, *Cognitive Disability Aesthetics: Visual Culture, Disability Representations, and the (in)visibility of Cognitive Difference* (Toronto: University of Toronto

Press, 2018) and the seminal work of Rosemarie Garland-Thomson, including "Seeing the Disabled: Visual Rhetorics of Disability in Popular Photography," in *The New Disability History: American Perspectives*, ed. Paul K. Longmore and Lauri Umansky (New York: New York University Press, 2001), 335–74, and "The Politics of Staring: Visual Rhetorics of Disability in Popular Photography," in *Disability Studies: Enabling the Humanities*, ed. Sharon L. Snyder, Rosemarie Garland Thomson, and Brenda Jo Brueggemann (Modern Language Association of America, 2002), 56–75.

24. For this whole series of thoughts about "visual evidence," see Michael Renov's *Subject of Documentary* (Minneapolis: University of Minnesota Press, 2004) in the groundbreaking series edited by him, Jane Gaines, and Faye Ginsburg.

25. Jennifer Bajorek starts us on this journey of "unfixing" photographs from dominant ways of seeing that structure our relationship with photography from/of the Global South (*Unfixed: Photography and Decolonial Imagination in West Africa* [Durham, NC: Duke University Press, 2020]). Also see Ariella Aïsha Azoulay, *Potential History: Unlearning Imperialism* (New York: Verso, 2019).

26. Abdelkebir al-Khatibi, "Double Critique," in *Plural Maghreb: Writings on Postcolonialism*, trans. Burcu Yalim (London: Bloomsbury, 2019), 30.

27. Ahmed, *Queer Phenomenology*, 41.

28. Jacques Rancière, *Dissensus: On Politics and Aesthetics*, trans. Steven Corcoran (London: Continuum, 2010), 69.

29. Decolonial and postcolonial methodologies regarding the visual and the aesthetic come from a broad spectrum of theorists. An insufficient sample includes theoretical studies of Blackness in the United States such as Fred Moten, *Black and Blur (consent not to be a single being)* (Durham, NC: Duke University Press, 2017) and Saidiya Hartman, *Wayward Lives, Beautiful Experiments: Intimate Histories of Social Upheaval* (New York: Norton, 2019). It might also include Walter Mignolo's concept of "aesthetic entanglements"; see Rubén Gaztambide-Fernández, "Decolonial Options and artistic/aetheSic entanglements: An Interview with Walter Mignolo," *Decolonization: Indigeneity, Education & Society* 3, no. 1 (2014): 196–212. Or scholars of the Middle East, South Asia, and Africa such as Ali Behdad, *Camera Orientalis: Reflections on Photography of the Middle East* (Chicago: University of Chicago Press, 2016); Stephen Sheehi, *Arab Imago: A Social History of Photographic Portraiture 1850–1910* (Princeton, NJ: Princeton University Press, 2016); Christopher Pinney, *Photography and Anthropology* (London: Reaktion, 2011) and Bajorek, *Unfixed*.

30. To think about the ways in which "theory" coopts and displaces not only people of color but also displaces modes and media of critical inquiry that are deemed otherwise not valuable or not "theoretical," see Barbara Christian, "The Race for Theory," *Feminist Studies* 14, no. 1 (Spring 1988): 67–79.

31. Amílcar Cabral, "Theory as a Weapon," *Unity and Struggle: Speeches and Writings of Amílcar Cabral*, trans.Michael Wolfers (New York: Monthly Review, 1979), 119–37.

32. Cabral, "Theory as a Weapon," 123, 120.

33. Jacques Rancière, *The Emancipated Spector*, trans. Gregory Elliot (New York, Verso, 2009), 13.

34. Stephen Sheehi, "From Sheikh Jarrah to Gaza: Palestine is Presence," *Journal of Visual Culture* (2022): 221–26.

35. Ali Behdad, *Camera Orientalis: Reflections on Photography of the Middle East* (Chicago: University of Chicago Press, 2016).

36. For a sample of works that discuss how Arab cultural producers "enacted" modernity in a variety of literary, architectural, visual and intellectual ways, see Tarek El-Ariss, *Trials of Arab Modernity: Literary Affects and the New Political* (New York: Fordham University Press, 2013); Wilson Chacko Jacob, *Working Out Egypt: Effendi Masculinity and Subject Formation in Colonial Modernity, 1870–1940* (Durham: Duke University Press, 2011); Stephen Sheehi, *Foundations of Modern Arab Identity* (Gainesville: University Press of Florida, 2004); Sheehi, *Arab Imago*; Keith Watenpaugh, *Being Modern in the Middle East: Revolution, Nationalism, Colonialism, and the Arab Middle Class* (Princeton, NJ: Princeton University Press, 2014).

37. For a more precise and developed explanation of the Osmanli or "Ottoman perspective" (*manzhar*), see Sheehi, *Arab Imago*, e.g. xxiii.

38. For a discussion of the portraiture in Jawhariyyeh's albums, see Stephen Sheehi, "Portrait Paths: Studio Photography in Ottoman Palestine," *Jerusalem Quarterly* 61 (2015): 23–41.

39. Walid Khalidi, *Before Their Diaspora: A Photographic History of the Palestinians* (Washington, DC: Institute for Palestine Studies, 1984).

40. Tina M. Campt, *Listening to Images* (Durham, NC: Duke University Press, 2017), 72.

41. Lena Meari, "Reconsidering Trauma: Towards a Palestinian Community Psychology," *Journal of Community Psychology* 43, no. 1 (2015): 76–86.

42. Naseeb Shaheen, *Pictorial History of Ramallah* (Beirut: Arab Institute for Research and Publishing, 1992), 8.

43. In addition to Campt's remarkable insights regarding the affective power of photography and the possibilities presented by that affect, Marianne Hirsch shows that family photographic albums in the United States supported accepted ideological configurations of the idealized family and society, the "familial gaze" as well as a familial look that accepts others into the family albums' narrative. See Marianne Hirsch, *Family Frames: Photography, Narrative, and Postmemory* (Cambridge, MA: Harvard University Press, 1997).

44. Constance Abdallah, *To Be a Palestinian: An Anthropology of One Man's Culture, The Life and Times of Hassan Mustafa Hassan Abdallah* (Chicago: Adam Writing and Publishing, 2000).

45. Salman Abu Sitta, *Mapping My Return: A Palestinian Memoir* (New York: American University of Cairo Press, 2017), x.

46. Raja Shehadeh, *Rift in Time: Travels with My Ottoman Uncle* (New York: OR Books, 2011).

47. Najib Khuri Nassar, *al-Sahuniyah: tarikhuha, gharaduha. hammiyatuha (Zionism: Its History, Its Goal. Its Priorities)* (Haifa: Matba'at al-Karmil, 1911). For a fine taxonomy of the book, see Emanuel Beška, "Arabic Translations of Writing on Zionism Published in Palestine before the First World War," *Asian and African Studies* 23, no. 1 (2014): 154–72.

48. Shehadeh, *Rift in Time*, 92.

49. The assertion that Jawhariyyeh established or imagined the first Palestinian national museum may be contested. Ilan Pappé relates that, around the turn of the century Ismail Musa al-Hussein, who had an erudite fascination with Palestinian antiquity, "began to collect ancient artifacts found by foreign archeologists" and "arranged [six of them] in a handsome permanent display at the Sultaniyah school opposite Herod's Gate." Pappé claims that "this was the first Palestinian museum" (*The Rise and Fall of a Palestinian Dynasty: The Husaynis, 1700–1948* [Berkeley: University of California Press, 2010], 107).

50. Jawhariyyeh, *Storyteller of Jerusalem*, 171.

51. Jawhariyyeh, *Storyteller of Jerusalem*, 125.

52. Jawhariyyeh, *Storyteller of Jerusalem*, 198.

53. Jawhariyyeh, *Storyteller of Jerusalem*, 201.

54. Jawhariyyeh, *Storyteller of Jerusalem*, 169.

55. Jawhariyyeh, *Storyteller of Jerusalem*, x, 172.

56. André Malraux, *Voices of Silence*, trans. Stuart Gilbert (St. Albans: Paladin, 1974).

57. Malraux, *Voices of Silence*, 14.

58. Azoulay, *Potential History*, 64.

59. Azoulay, *Potential History*, 65.

60. Jawhariyyeh, *Storyteller of Jerusalem*, 133

61. Jawhariyyeh, *Storyteller of Jerusalem*, 52.

62. Jawhariyyeh, *Storyteller of Jerusalem*, 62.

63. Martha Langford also discusses the role of photography albums in imagining or remembering history (*Suspended Conversations: The Afterlife of Memory in Photographic Albums* [Montreal: McGill-Queen University Press, 2001]). For a history of "photobooks," see Patrizia Di Bello, Colette Wilson and Shamoon Zamir, eds., *The Photobook from Talbot to Ruscha and Beyond* (London: I.B. Tauris, 2012). And for an insightful gendered reading of photo albums and women, see Patrizia Di Bello, *Women's Albums and Photography in Victorian England: Ladies, Mothers and Flirts* (Burlington, VT: Ashgate, 2007).

64. Georges Didi-Huberman, *Images in Spite of All: Four Photographs from Auschwitz*, trans. Shane B. Lillis (Chicago: University of Chicago Press, 2008), 151.

65. Sheehi, "Portrait Paths."

66. Jawhariyyeh, *Storyteller of Jerusalem*, 139.

67. Ruth Kark and Michal Oren-Nordheim, *Jerusalem and its Environs: Quarters, Neighborhoods, Villages, 1800–1948*, (Jerusalem: Hebrew University Press, 2001); 128

68. Roberto Mazza, Maria Chiara Rioli, and Stéphane Ancel, "The History of the Forgotten Diplomatic Mission, 1846–1940," *Jerusalem Quarterly*, Issue 71 (Autumn) 2017; 102.

69. Jawhariyyeh, *Storyteller of Jerusalem*, 139.

70. Jawhariyyeh, *Storyteller of Jerusalem*, 139.

71. Jawhariyyeh, *Storyteller of Jerusalem*, 140.

72. Jacques Rancière, *Politics of Aesthetics: Distribution of the Sensible*, translated by Gabriel Rockhill (London: Continuum, 2004); 12.

73. Rancière, *Politics of Aesthetics*, 12.

74. Georges Didi-Huberman, *Confronting Images: Questioning the Ends of a Certain History of Art*, trans. John Goodman (University Park, PA: Penn State University Press, 2005), xxii.

75. Georges Didi-Huberman, "The Surviving Image: Aby Warburg and Tylorian Anthropology," *Oxford Art Journal* 25, no. 1 (2002): 61.

76. Didi-Huberman, "The Surviving Image," 68.

77. Didi-Huberman, *The Surviving Image*, 26.

78. Among many publications see Steven Salaita, *Inter/Nationalism: Decolonizing Native America and Palestine* (Minneapolis: University of Minnesota Press, 2016) and J. Kehaulani Kauanui, *Speaking of Indigenous Politics: Conversations with Activists, Scholars, and Tribal Leaders* (Minneapolis: University of Minnesota Press, 2018).

79. Rancière, *Dissensus*, 39.

80. Rancière, *Dissensus*, 39.

81. Rana Barakat, "The Jerusalem Fellah: Popular Politics in Mandate-Era Palestine," *Journal of Palestine Studies* XLVI, no. 1 (Autumn 2016): 8. For the aftermath of the Buraq revolt, see Rana Barakat, "Criminals or Martyrs? Let the Courts Decide!—British Colonial Legacy in Palestine and the Criminalization of Resistance," *Al-Muntaqa* 1, no. 1 (2018): 84–97.

82. Julie Peteet, *Gender in Crisis: Women and the Palestinian Resistance Movement* (New York: Columbia University Press, 2010), 43. Also see Ellen Fleischmann, *The Nation and Its "New" Women: The Palestinian Women's Movement 1920–1948* (Berkeley: University of California, 2003).

83. Peteet, *Gender in Crisis*, 48.

84. Matiel Moghannam's autobiography, as quoted by Peteet, *Gender in Crisis*, 47. For the first-person account in English, see Matiel Moghannam, *The Arab Woman and the Palestine Problem* (London: Herbert Joseph, 1937).

85. Fleischmann, *The Nation and Its "New" Women*, 117. Moghannam's autobiography features prominently in Fleischmann's study, which approaches it with critical but respectful discernment. See, e.g. *The Nation and Its "New" Women*, 117–22.

86. In addition to Peteet's and Fleischmann's histories, see Mogannam, *The Arab Woman*, and Anbara Salam al-Khalidi, *Memoirs of an Early Arab Feminist: The Life and Activism of Anbara Salam Khalidi*, trans. Tarif Khalidi (London: Pluto, 2013).

87. For a clear and compelling introduction to social reproduction theory see Tithi Bhattacharya, ed., *Social Reproduction Theory: Remapping Class, Recentring Oppression* (London: Pluto, 2017); Silvia Federici, *Revolution at Point Zero: Housework, Reproduction, and Feminist Struggle* (Oakland, CA: PM Press, 2012); and Nancy Fraser's sharp and concise "Contradictions of Capital and Care," *New Left Review* 100 (July/Aug 2016): 99–117, https://newleftreview.org/issues/ii100/articles/nancy-fraser-contradictions-of-capital-and -care.

88. Prominent members of the Executive Committee hailed from families that were the backbone of the Palestinian ruling class, all of whom appear in Jawhariyyeh's photographs: Fatima al Husseini, Khadija al-Husseini, Tarab 'Abd al-Hadi, Wahida al-Khalidi, Diya al-Nashashibi, Zahiyah Nashashibi, Ni'mati 'Alami, Katrin Dib, Shahinda Duzdar, Anisa al-Khadra, Melia Sakakini, Zulaykha Shihabi, Mary Shahadah, and Sa'adiyah al-'Alami. For a fine study on their activism, see Ellen Fleischmann, "The Emergence of the Palestinian Women's Movement, 1929–1939," *Journal of Palestine Studies* 29, no. 3 (2000): 16–32.

89. Tali Hatuka, "Negotiating Space: Analyzing Jaffa Protest Form, Intention, and Violence, October 27, 1933," *Jerusalem Quarterly* 35 (2008): 95.

90. Hatuka, "Negotiating Space," 99.

91. Hatuka, "Negotiating Space," 96.

92. Rashid Khalidi, *The Iron Cage: The Story of the Palestinian Struggle for Statehood* (Oxford: Oneworld, 2006), 88–90.

93. Khalidi, *The Iron Cage*, 89.

94. Rancière, *Politics of Aesthetics*, 13.

6. EPILOGUE: THE PRESENCE AND POTENTIAL OF PALESTINE

1. Edward Said and Jean Mohr, *After the Last Sky: Palestinian Lives* (New York: Pantheon Books, 1986), 88.

2. Said and Mohr, *After the Last Sky*, 88.

3. Philip Gourevitch and Errol Morris, *The Ballad of Abu Ghraib* (New York: Penguin Books, 2009), 148, cited in Jennifer Tucker, "Entwined Practices: Engagements with Photography in Historical Inquiry," *History and Theory* 48, no. 4 (2009): 1.

4. Ariella Azoulay, *Potential History: Unlearning Imperialism* (New York: Verso, 2019). Also, see her "Potential History: Thinking through Violence," in *Critical Inquiry* 39, no. 3 (Spring 2013): 565.

5. Ariella Azoulay, *The Civil Contract of Photography* (New York: Zone Books, 2008), 14.

6. Peter Gran, *Rise of the Rich: A New View of Modern History* (Syracuse, NY: Syracuse University Press, 2009), 60.

7. Sherene Seikaly, *Men of Capital: Scarcity and Economy in Mandate Palestine* (Stanford, CA: Stanford University Press, 2015).

8. Muhammad Muslih, *The Origins of Palestine Nationalism* (New York: Columbia University Press, 1988), 164–65.

9. Ilan Pappé, *The Rise and Fall of a Palestinian Dynasty: The Husaynis, 1700–1948* (Berkeley: University of California Press, 2010), 90.

10. Pappé, *The Husaynis*, 128–32.

11. Rana Barakat, "The Jerusalem Fellah: Popular Politics in Mandate-Era Palestine," *Journal of Palestine Studies* XLVI, no. 1 (Autumn 2016): 7–19; Seikaly, *Men of Capital*.

12. Parcellation Scheme of Wasif Jahariyyah, 1910/31, Scheme number 568, Government of Palestine, Jerusalem District Building and Town Planning Commission, Israel National Archives.

13. Michael Jensen, "Fence is Gone, There is Still Partition," *Jordan Times*, May 22, 2018, https://archive.fo/20150201104709/ http://jordantimes.com/fence-is-gone-there-is-still -partition#selection-1271.24–1271.137.

14. Rana Barakat, "Mujimun am shuhuda'? Fa-linada' al-mahkamah tuqariru! Al-Irth al-'isti'mari al-Britani fi Falistin wa tajrim al-muqawimah," *'Umran* (Omran) 2, no. 6 (Autumn 2013): 33–54; Barakat, "The Jerusalem Fellah."

15. Beshara Doumani, *Rediscovering Palestine: Merchants and Peasants in Jabal Nablus, 1700–1900* (Berkeley: University of California Press, 1995), 7.

16. Some of these scholars who have been re-shaping our understanding of Mandate Palestine include Lauren Banko, Rana Barakat, Beshara Doumani, Laura Robson, Sherene Seikaly, Andrea Stanton, and Salim Tamari.

17. Rana Barakat, "Writing/righting Palestine Studies: Settler Colonialism, Indigenous Sovereignty and Resisting the Ghost(s) of History," *Settler Colonial Studies* 8, no. 3 (2018): 201, 353.

18. Barakat, "Writing/righting Palestine Studies," 355.

19. Barakat, "Writing/righting Palestine Studies," 360.

INDEX

Founded in 1893,
UNIVERSITY OF CALIFORNIA PRESS
publishes bold, progressive books and journals
on topics in the arts, humanities, social sciences,
and natural sciences—with a focus on social
justice issues—that inspire thought and action
among readers worldwide.

The UC PRESS FOUNDATION
raises funds to uphold the press's vital role
as an independent, nonprofit publisher, and
receives philanthropic support from a wide
range of individuals and institutions—and from
committed readers like you. To learn more, visit
ucpress.edu/supportus.

9 780520 382886